KNOW THE GAME, PLAY THE GAME

DEVELOPING A CAREER IN A MULTINATIONAL FIRM

... And How to Get There in the First Place

by Larry Wang

1/03

Clemson,
Enjoy the book!
Larry Wang

ANDIREMAR PUBLICATIONS

Published in China by:

CHINA TRANSLATION & PUBLISHING CORPORATION

Floor 6, Wuhua Building
4 (A) Chegongzhuang Street
West District, Beijing 100044, China

Design/Cover: George Ngan/New Strategy
Illustrations: Henry Wong
Layout: Polly Yu Production Ltd

Printed and bound in China

TO BRENDA,
WHOSE INPUT, ENCOURAGEMENT, AND ENTHUSIASM TO SEE THIS BOOK
FINISHED I FELT EVERY STEP OF THE WAY.

Author's Notes
... Some Important Clarifications

Before you begin, there are a few points that I would like to clarify about the contents of this book. The most important is that readers should not have the expectation that this book will help them determine which industries, companies, or careers they should be pursuing. This book does not advise readers on which computer programming languages are most beneficial to learn these days, on how to become a management consultant, or on whether marketing or finance is a better career track.

Rather than these "hard skills," this book focuses on the "soft skills" that are very necessary for developing a successful career in a multinational company operating in China. Its aim is to provide guidance and insight that will help readers develop a mature, professional approach to their job search and career development, so that when they do find themselves facing critical situations related to their career, they will be better prepared to make good decisions.

In addition, I would like to note that most of the professionals and executives interviewed in this book are based in Shanghai and Beijing. Therefore, the anecdotes and stories that follow are drawn from the experiences of those working in these two major cities. It was not my intent to exclude the work experiences of those in other mainland cities. Logistics and access to resources created limitations. However, I believe the job-seeking and career development advice are just as applicable to mainland professionals working in other locations throughout China as well.

Also, when I use the term mainland professional throughout the book, I am referring to those mainlanders who have neither had the opportunity to study nor work abroad (those would fall under the category of mainland-born returnees, or MBRs). Therefore, their personal and professional backgrounds do not include the experience of having lived in a different country.

Finally, the names of many of the people who are quoted and talked about in this book have been changed. They were quite honest and candid with their comments while being interviewed, and wished to avoid any sensitivities within their company and with the people they deal with. Their situations and viewpoints, however, are quite real and reflective of what they experience when encountering job search, career development, and management issues in China.

Acknowledgments

Writing this book has been an enjoyable and beneficial process for me personally, particularly the opportunity to speak in depth with many interesting people about their perspectives and experiences working and developing their careers in China. Today, they are friends and sources of insight, information, and inspiration regarding the evolving capabilities and outstanding potential of mainland professionals.

For their role in enhancing the messages and presentation of the words in this book, I'd like to thank Henry Wong for his artwork and images, George Ngan for the cover design and Polly Yu for her book layout work.

I'd also like to thank the readers who helped provide invaluable feedback on some very unpolished early drafts, particularly my dad, Daniel Wang; my mom, Virginia Li; and my sister, Caroline Wang.

Finally, I'd like to especially thank all my colleagues at Wang & Li who helped review and critique the book, and gave their full support to this project: Mina Li, Gemma Lim, Linda Liu, Annie Pan, Chris Han, Jessie Wang, Tina Wang, and Joan Xu. And my utmost appreciation to Sue Song, who in addition, assisted in the coordination and production of the entire book process.

Contents

Contents

Introduction

The New China

If you meet Steven Song in person, or even speak with him by phone, you would swear that he spent a good many years of his life outside of Mainland China. By any measure of international standards, he is confident, articulate, well presented, and able to communicate comfortably and effectively in English. Steven is 30 years old and is the director of sales for Nortel Networks in Beijing, responsible for developing global alliance agreements between newly licensed mainland telecommunications carriers and international carriers. Steven also happens to be 100 percent, born and raised Mainland Chinese. He has never before lived or worked abroad.

Steven's international demeanor comes partly from his father, who studied in England as a visiting scholar early in his career. However, when asked how he acquired such an open manner of communication and thinking, Steven credits a different source. "While working in Shanghai, I spent a lot of time after work and on weekends in pubs," he describes. "I learn a lot just by hanging out and speaking with my western colleagues about business, the economy, sports, cars, or even dating. Besides being interesting to talk to, I'm able to gain an understanding about business and the outside world from them."

Beyond just his strong sales performance, Steven stands out in other ways to his company's management. "Steven has a fantastic ability to break down barriers between Chinese and foreigners. He's an excellent communicator, not just in what he says, but in capturing the gist of what is being talked about," says James Burton, the general manager who hired Steven for his first job as a sales assistant with GPT, Britain's largest telecommunications manufacturer. "He's also extremely proactive and can always find a way through a problem to get the job done. That's an ability we wish more of our mainland staff had."

For employers like James Burton, the future is clear. "When multinationals talk about the ideal employee for their China operations, they're really talking about people like Steven Song," says James. "Steven is, 'The New China.'"

An Exceptional Time

"At no time has there existed such opportunities in China for mainland professionals." That's what a woman in Shanghai emphasized while being interviewed. Her statement came before I even had a chance to reveal to her my theme for this book, or my insights about the outstanding career picture today for mainland professionals. Talk about someone stealing your thunder.

But I was glad she said it. She was exactly right. China's surging economy is creating tremendous, long-awaited chances for multinationals bold and smart enough to meet the demands of its rapidly maturing markets. New products, services, and technologies that are helping to improve the quality of life, raise living standards, and facilitate greater economic advancement are pouring into the mainland from abroad. To grow and succeed, the multinationals that are bringing to China these things are in dire need of well-qualified professional staff.

Today, however, multinationals no longer wish to build their management teams with high-priced, foreign expatriates who have limited ability to operate effectively in China. Instead, they seek professionals with "one foot in the East and one foot in the West." They want people who possess the best of both worlds in terms of language skills, education, cultural understanding, and professional training, who can apply world-class business practices to local markets. As a result, the timing for Mainland Chinese professionals is excellent. For those with bilingual skills and international-oriented business backgrounds, in particular, exceptional career opportunities are available.

Undeniable Trend

Undeniably, China's home-grown professional talent is maturing rapidly. More and more, mainlanders are evolving into key management roles by demonstrating the caliber of business skills that multinational firms seek. "The Mainland Chinese graduates I meet are among the best I've seen in the region. They're as good or better than ones from Hong Kong, Taiwan, or Singapore," says Mei Wong, a former partner at Tasa International, a top executive search firm in Hong Kong. At Tasa, Mei specialized in recruiting local Chinese managers for multinationals operating in China. "They're extremely smart, hard working, and motivated. What they tend to lack is just one ingredient; exposure. But that is changing quickly and happening for many, even as we speak."

The "exposure" that multinational managers allude to is also commonly referred to as "polish," "finesse," or "insight." It is the intangible qualities that demonstrate themselves through strong communication, business sense, initiative, problem solving skills, and an understanding of international business practices and management thinking. It is the strength of these qualities that makes a candidate suitable for multinationals and their business style, and that allows these companies to be aggressive and strategic in their approach to developing their operation in the mainland.

Ultimately, it is the new generation of mainland professionals who are the acknowledged solution for expanding multinationals with staffing needs in China. They are fitting the bill and providing the type and caliber of business skills being sought. Currently, however, the supply of well-trained ones falls far short of the demand. It's not that there aren't enough Mainland Chinese who are capable and willing enough. There are. But most don't yet have the scope of professional training and experience required by multinationals to take on key roles. Mei predicts that this will change dramatically within the next three to five years.

"The advantages that internationally trained professionals offer multinational firms still exist for the most part," Mei continues. "For instance, with limited overseas exposure, local mainland professionals have greater difficulty communicating and managing expectations with both regional and home office executives. They also tend not to be as strong in their ability to plan and think strategically, and to see the big picture in terms of long-term, company-wide objectives. However, the areas where overseas-trained professionals have typically had an advantage over local professionals are becoming fewer and fewer. The first wave of mainland professionals have been working in multinationals only for the past five to ten years. But many will soon have the years of experience with leading international companies that you want your upper middle to senior managers to have."

With the playing field wide open to anyone able to get results in China's constantly evolving business environment, it is a fortuitous time for mainland professionals to step into those critical positions that multinational firms must fill. The issue isn't so much where to find the opportunities, but how to attain them.

Why I Wrote This Book

Know The Game, Play The Game takes a fundamental approach to what it takes to develop a successful career in a multinational company. Like any game that you participate in, the more you understand the rules, the better sense you have for the game's strategy, and the more you can anticipate the moves of the players involved, then the greater your chances are for succeeding. This is the initial challenge for many mainland professionals who are seeking opportunities or greater roles within multinational companies. They wish to participate in a business environment that is relatively new to them, but don't yet have the insights into what multinational executives value most with regards to an employee's capabilities and promotability. They have had limited exposure to the corporate environments and management practices that they must understand better in order to develop the right type of skills and professional habits to succeed.

Of course, the easiest advice to give someone wishing to gain world-class business and management skills is to obtain an MBA from abroad, preferably from a well-known institution such as Harvard, Wharton, Stanford, or some other world-class business school program. This is certainly an attractive option for those fortunate enough to be able to study overseas. But how many mainlanders have the money or resources to afford such an investment? For the overwhelming majority, this is not a realistic solution.

That's why I've written this book. It's for those mainland professionals who need another alternative to gaining a deeper understanding of the multinational corporate world, and to acquiring international capabilities and perspectives through the resources available to them here in China. Although the career development opportunities that a multinational firm can offer are excellent, getting there is a high hurdle to clear for many. And once inside, advancement to top management positions is a real challenge. This book shares those insights into how multinational companies operate and how their senior management teams think. It provides practical advice that makes the prospect of finding a job and developing a career with a multinational company more accessible.

Fortunately, with far more footsteps to follow today, knowing how to attain a promising position and develop one's career is much easier compared to just a few years ago. Increasingly, there are examples like Steven Song who are optimizing the opportunities available to them and making themselves highly desirable to multinational firms. The experiences that this book shares come from mainland professionals who have never before worked or studied abroad. Yet, they are successfully advancing their careers in leading international companies. They've either done it the smart way, or learned it the hard way.

This book also addresses basic, but difficult to answer issues that hold back many from attaining an attractive opportunity. It identifies key skills that international managers seek, and provides job search advice to help you pursue attractive openings. It highlights the realities you'll encounter, such as higher performance standards, cultural adjustments, and new business practices. From the anecdotes shared, I believe you will be able to relate to many of the situations I have written about.

Who Am I?

Before continuing, I have a confession to make. I am not mainland Chinese. Well actually, I am, in a way. My dad is from Shanghai and my mom is from Guangzhou. But I was born and raised in the United States. My grandparents went to the U.S. from China over 50 years ago. In doing so, they left behind virtually everything they owned. As immigrants, they embarked on a journey over the next several decades that is somewhat familiar to many Chinese American families. My maternal grandparents started a series of Chinese restaurants. The first was a modest chop suey and chow mein shop in New York City. Within a few years, they opened one of the first and most successful Chinese restaurants to introduce traditional, gourmet Chinese cuisine to the U.S. In its day, "it was the place to be seen within New York's social circle," according to my aunt.

Meanwhile, their children — my parents, aunts, and uncles — studied hard and attended the best universities. Later, they pursued worthy vocations. Over the years, the masters and doctoral degrees accumulated and the achievements as academics, doctors, lawyers, and civil servants mounted. In turn, their hard work and perseverance resulted in a comfortable life and further opportunities for their children (my brother, sister, cousins, and me).

Oddly, I have returned to the place where my parents and grandparents left five decades ago. My life in the U.S. was prosperous and enjoyable. However, I have come to Asia, and now China, for clear reasons. It is a place where I can share the best of what I have to offer as someone who is parts Chinese and parts western. I believe it is in China, at this time, where my background can be best applied and where I can attain my most meaningful professional and personal rewards.

Personal Travelogue

Why I Came To Greater China

My first trip to Asia was in September of 1985. I was 25 years old. My brother and I accompanied our grandmother back to Mainland China for a seven city tour. It was only her second visit back in almost 40 years. She was 72 at the time.

Although we came along to take care of her, it quickly became apparent during the trip that she had far more stamina and energy than we did. She was the one who ended up taking care of us! There's a picture I have of her and me sitting on the back of a camel. The picture was taken on a sand dune in Dunhuang, one of the western most cities in inner China. I'm sitting in front looking a bit off-balanced and unnerved. My grandmother is sitting behind me, peering off into the distance with a look of anticipation. In a nutshell, that was my grandma.

The trip was highly memorable for many other reasons. China was just opening up at the time. There was an early spattering of blue jeans, colorful fashions, and western consumer goods. For the most part, however, the flavor of everything we saw was distinctly Chinese. Blue and gray straight-legged suits were the standard dress. The people we met were rustic and weathered. The overall tempo of life was slow and relaxed, as pedestrians and bicyclers set the pace within the cities and villages we visited. The entire character and flavor of the country was very much as I had imagined.

Throughout the tour, I remember feeling completely humbled. I sensed real admiration from the people I met over the fact that I was a Chinese person who also happened to be an American. My grandparents and parents were able to immigrate to the U.S. For that reason alone, through no doing of my own, I had unlimited opportunities and dreams to pursue. Most of those I met did not. That made a deep impression on me. From that point on, I knew I would someday return to Asia. I hoped to participate in some way in the development of Chinese people and society. Five years later I moved to Greater China.

What makes me qualified to write this book?

I'd also like to mention that I am not a newcomer to Asia. In September of 2000, I passed my ten year anniversary out here. In January 1994, I founded a recruiting firm, Wang & Li Asia Resources, that supports the interests and opportunities of bilingual, international-oriented professionals throughout Greater China. Wang & Li specializes in placing this fast growing niche of candidates within international firms who are actively seeking such talent. Our success stems from our unique recruitment approach that places an emphasis on the creation and dissemination of career planning and job search advice. Beyond serving as just recruitment consultants, we are career development specialists who provide reliable information and services to professionals on job market, industry, and hiring trends in Greater China. Since our inception, we've advised and placed thousands of local, Asia-born returnee, and overseas Chinese who are playing significant roles in the success of both multinational firms and the region's overall emergence.

Actually, this book is a sequel to my first book, *The New Gold Mountain,* which I completed in May of 1998. It tells the story of the widening presence in Greater China of Chinese Americans, another category of bilingual, international-oriented professionals, who are leveraging their dual backgrounds and realizing outstanding success. *The New Gold Mountain* provides a first-hand look at the road many Chinese American professionals have taken to come to and do exceptionally well out here. By sharing their experiences and insights, it offers the best information available on how to find a job and develop a career in the region. It is this career development and job search advisory experience working with professionals who possess similar bilingual and international backgrounds and qualities that allows me to provide equally helpful guidance to mainland professionals wishing to work for a multinational firm.

This book is not about selling the virtues of international training or the superiority of multinational companies. I do, however, make a basic assumption: that multinational firms offer an excellent environment for mainland professionals who wish to develop highly desirable professional skills and realize excellent career opportunities. Through this book, I hope that many mainlanders will come to realize the personal, professional, and financial goals they are striving for.

Part I

Multinational Firms

Chapter 1 Where East Meets West

W hen visiting a friend in Shanghai in 1996, I recall walking around the city one Saturday afternoon. In terms of international foods, consumer products, entertainment, or conveniences, there was relatively little to be found. There were no Mister Donuts or Haagen Daz ice cream shops. There were no Ikea furniture and housewares, or Hallmark gifts and cards to buy. There were no Nike or The Athlete's Foot stores, or shopping malls filled with international retailers and brands.

How things have changed in a few short years. The cosmopolitan aspects and quality of life in major China cities have evolved dramatically. Today, western-style indoor shopping centers, like The Westgate Mall and CITIC Square in Shanghai and The Oriental Plaza and The China World Shopping Center in Beijing, offer a variety of popular international retail stores and boutiques to buy from, such as Burberry's, Espirit, Gucci, Hugo Boss, Nine West, Valentino, and Nautica. Mobile phones and pagers are commonplace among the general population. Personal computers and the Internet are standard tools for mainland students and professionals. You can buy Oreo cookies, Gatorade, and Corn Flakes in any supermarket or convenience store. You can eat at The Hard Rock Café, Tony Roma's, T.G.I. Friday's, The Rain Forest Café, or a number of other foreign restaurants. Or if you crave fast-food, you're sure to find a McDonald's, Kentucky Fried Chicken, Pizza Hut, A&W, or Subway. And now, even internationally famous Starbuck's has landed in China in full force, rolling out its chain of shops and brand of coffee culture among the growing cadre of mainland yuppies.

New Kids On The Block

Yes, multinationals are ramping up their efforts to service the maturing mainland consumer market. And they are doing it with a sense of urgency. Although they have established themselves as worldwide industry leaders over decades of offering leading products, services, expertise, and technologies to consumers and businesses internationally, their history is in China relatively short. Most are without the long-standing presence and relationships that Chinese companies have. Therefore, to win mainland business and market share, multinationals must move aggressively and offer the most compelling products and services available. They must also distinguish themselves on the basis of superior service, value, and quality.

In doing these things, the expertise and business practices that multinationals are bringing to the mainland are raising the performance and quality standards across every industry. To operate effectively, bilingual staff with well-rounded, high caliber business backgrounds are needed. Unfortunately, the supply of such professionals in China does not meet the demand at present. The resulting shortage is offering an unprecedented level of opportunities for those with the right combination of skills at the professional and management ranks.

Chapter 2   Outstanding Career Development Opportunities

$\mathbf{W}$hy do the outstanding career opportunities emphasized in this book revolve around multinational firms, when there are many Chinese companies that are significant, even dominant players within their industry?

Appreciation Of Skills

To begin with, the corporate cultures and business practices of multinationals in China are internationally oriented. Many in their management teams have been educated abroad and have worked within leading companies from around the world. They are able to offer the type of team building, strategic thinking, industry expertise, consultative problem solving approach, and management leadership that is highly beneficial for an employee's career development. This is not usually the case in Chinese companies where managers have developed their careers in less dynamic, less competitive environments.

Greater Exposure And Responsibility

With enormous opportunities before them, multinationals are aggressively growing their organizations, capturing market share, and building brand awareness in China.

Executing with speed is crucial, as nobody wants to play a catch-up game a few years down the road, when it will be too late.

The rapid expansion by these companies is creating tremendous career openings for anyone who can perform and get results. Mainland professionals are getting chances to take on responsibilities that they would not normally have to the same degree, or at the same stage in their careers, if in a state-owned enterprise (SOE). Where there is often the expectation to wait your turn in an SOE, management bottlenecks are not found as often in multinational firms that are short on highly qualified middle to senior level managers.

This is why you find younger professionals in multinational firms handling a greater scope of responsibilities. Performers are given chances to be involved in key areas and projects, despite little previous experience in what they're asked to do. This may include setting up new business operations, introducing new products or services, or evaluating new markets. The result is a steep learning curve, and opportunities to shine and move quickly up the career ladder for motivated, capable professionals.

One executive described the challenge in hiring qualified staff in this way: "There's tremendous pressure to grow the business and enter new markets. To do that you need excellent people. With few well-trained specialists out here though, it's not always the case that you're hiring the best person for a position. Frequently, you're hiring the best you can find."

In The Spotlight

If you're someone who wants to see how good you are and how high you can go, a multinational firm is the place to test yourself. Given their flatter corporate structures, management is usually more accessible. Younger staff often work closely with senior managers. With more interaction, there are more opportunities to both learn and have your contributions recognized. Mainly, if you're good at what you do, you'll stand out.

International Exposure

Most multinationals in China also offer chances for staff to travel abroad and gain invaluable international exposure. They can offer regional training opportunities and business trips to overseas offices. Overall, access to their broad, global resources are encouraged by multinationals, who understand its importance in the career development of promising managers.

Faster Career Advancement
It's Performance That Counts

Perhaps most attractive is the performance-driven environment that multinationals offer. Many mainland companies have traditional, hierarchical structures that favor longevity and company standing among employees. Young, hungry staff often find themselves in situations where managers who have been in the same company for twenty years or more have little interest in seeing someone advance to their level in half the time or less. In comparison, many managers in multinational firms are strikingly young. For these companies, career advancement is weighted heavily on one criteria; an ability to produce results.

If Your Company Doesn't Value You, Others Will

Finally, what ensures advancement for strong performers in China is the highly aggressive hiring nature of multinational companies themselves. My firm is part of the recruitment or "headhunting" industry, where the practice of headhunting candidates from one company to another has taken on new heights in the mainland. With a constant demand for, but insufficient pool of management talent, it's a hot field that will remain so as long as multinational firms here continue their pace of growth. Therefore, for qualified professionals, the hiring market is in your favor. If your company does not recognize your contributions and value, another company will. Your assurance is the active headhunting practices of recruitment firms in China.

The Multinational Company Experience

If you wish to take a less aggressive, more conservative approach to your career, then working in an international company is probably not the right fit for you. However, if you are the proactive type who wants to maximize your chances for exposure and growth, then a multinational firm can offer exciting opportunities that are both personally and professionally rewarding. The international exposure, promotional tracks, and chance to develop well-rounded, world-class business skills are major reasons why so many pursue a multinational career track. As one person put it: "With the globalization of world economies and the increasing competitiveness in the job market, would you rather be someone with international-oriented training and work experience, or without it?"

Part II

The Employment Situation

Chapter 3 The Situation: China's Rapidly Changing Business Environment

It is referred to as the Pacific Century, the Asia Century, or the Asia Miracle. These names all allude to the phenomenal economic emergence of the Asia Pacific region. In his 1996 #1 international best-selling book, *Megatrends Asia*, author and world-renowned trends forecaster John Naisbitt wrote:

Globalization is the phenomenon of the 21st century and the dominant region will be Asia. What is happening in Asia is by far the most important development in the world today. Nothing else comes close. Not only for Asians but the entire planet. The economic growth in Asia will drive the global economy to the benefit of us all as we move through the balance of this century. The modernization of Asia will forever re-shape the world as we move towards the next millennium.

Biggest, Fastest, Greatest

Within the region, China's economy is leading the charge and drawing unprecedented numbers of companies, investment, and resources to the mainland. Every multinational marketing presentation echoes the same facts; nearly 1.3 billion consumers and the world's fastest growing economy over the past 15 years. Since the early 1990's, China has been the world's second leading destination, only behind the United States, for international investment.

Of course, the primary catalyst for growth has been the dramatic increase in the purchasing power of mainland consumers and households hungry for items ranging from ice cream, VCD and DVD players, and athletic shoes, to mobile phones, soft drinks, and cosmetics. A recent survey by the State Statistical Bureau shows that the average annual income of urban families within the 10 largest mainland cities was RMB6,000 (US$725), compared to only one-fourth of all families earning that much just five years ago. Increasing income levels have also placed a greater emphasis on quality of life and leisure, creating a yearning for entertainment, media, travel, and sports. In so many areas, untapped markets are opening up as fast as new products and services can be introduced to the country.

For instance, China's cosmetics industry is expected to grow by over 20 percent annually, to between US$7 and 8 billion by the year 2003. China's number of phone users already exceeds 250 million, with over 40 percent of those being mobile subscribers, whose numbers are growing exponentially. Internet users are projected to grow to over 150 million by the end of 2005, and will eventually make up the largest on-line user-base in the world. And in response to these kinds of market increases, China's advertising industry has grown at an annual rate of 39.7 percent since 1991, with annual turnover of RMB71.2 billion (US$8.6 billion) at the end of 2000. These are the types of numbers being contemplated by multinationals aiming to become significant players in the mainland.

Although occurring with stops and starts, China's standard of living is improving faster and for more people than anywhere in the world. With multinationals targeting it as their next major market, a high stakes game is being played. Some are even banking their future on their success in the mainland, which could catapult them into a world leadership position. For multinational firms eager to develop their mainland business, China's time has arrived.

New Industries, Companies, And Skill Sets
Suddenly Services
With the dash to win China's consumer market has come an influx of new industries that are expanding quickly and having a major impact in elevating the country's economy. Growing particularly fast are commercial and consumer service ones. For example, as recently as six years ago, consulting was not much of a concept, let alone a business practice in China. However, today there is a strong demand by companies needing outside help, that wish to establish new operations or expand existing ones. Similarly, the skyrocketing usage of information technology among users and businesses only began over the past few years. The explosion in media and entertainment has happened only over the past four to five years as well. Marketing, communications, advertising, and public relations firms have also emerged in response to the aggressive business development activities of many growing businesses.

At the same time, huge amounts of money are being invested into China infrastructure projects, manufacturing facilities, and business operations. Since the early 1990s, financial services like investment banking and corporate finance have emerged to provide the capital that is making much of the expansion possible, by allowing local companies to list in international investment markets. Meanwhile, legal and accountancy services have also grown to help protect the interests and measure the results of foreign participants investing in the mainland.

Multinationals On The Move
Common among these service and service-related industries are their international origins. They are businesses that have all evolved and matured abroad. As a result, their emergence in China has been paralleled by the appearance of multinationals who have entered the mainland in a major way. Many have been innovators in their field and established themselves as worldwide industry leaders over several decades.

Their presence in China, however, is relatively new. For example, Microsoft, arguably the world's leading information technology company, established its operation in China in the mid-1990s, while Dell Computers only set up here in 1996. And consider McKinsey & Company and the Boston Consulting Group, two of the leading names in consulting. They only established their China practices in the early 1990s.

In consumer products and consumer services, Kentucky Fried Chicken and Nike are global household names. Yet it was only in the mid-1990s that they began making a concerted effort to grow their China business. Kentucky Fried Chicken opened its first store in Beijing in 1994. Today, over 400 stores serve the Chinese population. In 1995, Nike opened its first retail store in Shanghai. Now, the city has over 25 stores. In essence, these and hundreds of other international firms are all cranking up their efforts in China in unison.

In It For The Long Haul

Although many multinationals have yet to make money in the mainland (with some still losing very big), they are not holding back. Their outlook for becoming a leading player in China is a long-term one. With tremendous amounts of money and resources already sunk into business operations and market development, they remain committed and optimistic over their future in China. As an indication, more and more companies have moved their China headquarters from Hong Kong to Shanghai and Beijing in recent years. They are even extending key operations and sales offices far beyond major cities, to remote locations where they are closer to markets and where operating costs are lower.

New Skills

These fast growing, market-hungry multinationals have sparked the demand for international-caliber professional skills. Consumer product companies are launching products into new markets as quickly as they can identify people to manage those lines of business. These companies must understand local customer needs, deliver compelling product messages to consumers, and establish retail and distribution channels. To do this, they require managers with marketing, brand management, product development, sales management, and channel management capabilities.

The expansion of business operations across China has also increased the necessity and demand of timely, reliable information. Not only are information systems management skills needed, but systems integration, information technology (IT) consulting, and applications development expertise are also in demand. Technology firms, in general, are all on the lookout for project managers, pre- and post-sales support staff, and systems analysts who can design, implement, and oversee evolving technologies.

Tracking the financial health of such joint ventures and regional operations, and determining the viability of existing and potential projects requires the involvement of finance managers, controllers, and auditors. And to assist companies with market entry and new business initiatives, a range of consultants with strategic planning, market research, general management, and process improvement experience are in demand.

Unfortunately, as with the industries they serve, most of these professional skills are not innate to the mainland. Rather, they have been nurtured and practiced abroad for years within Fortune 1000 corporate cultures and top international business school programs. Within China, however, such capabilities and expertise have had a limited presence.

New Way Of Doing Business

For many reasons, multinational companies have not found doing business in China an easy game to play. For most, early approaches to the mainland market have not produced the expected results. These have included an over reliance on inside connections to win deals and a lack of commitment to developing local resources and skills. Over the years, many have claimed to know someone who is the key to delivering the China market. Although you can never have too many connections in China, enough companies have learned costly lessons by counting on relationships alone. Beyond just having an inside track, what makes a partnership or venture fruitful is the ability to implement business plans and manage projects effectively.

As a result, multinationals are no longer satisfied with just being able to strike deals and identify relationships. Instead, the emphasis has shifted to the follow-through and the ability to execute. A greater focus is being placed on the implementation of international management techniques and business expertise, such as strong customer service, product quality, marketing, project management, and strategic planning activities. The increased presence of multinationals, overall, is raising the mainland's professional standards across all industries.

Higher Expectations

Yesterday's Approach: Investing For The Future

Finally, the business approach and expectations of multinationals towards China has evolved considerably over recent years. When they first began in China, the mainland was a black hole. It was a far away, exotic place to foreign companies. Not much was known about the people, culture, or how to do business here. However, one thing was known. China's market had great potential.

Although strategies were not well-defined, multinationals knew they should be operating in China in some capacity. The initial approach was a long-term investment one. To get to know the market, offices were set up to conduct early business development activities. Although operations lost money each year, the emphasis was to establish a foundation so that when the market potential turned real, they would be ready to participate in the boom.

Today's Approach: Make Some Money!

As the long awaited spending among China's consumers has arrived, so has a change in the business objective for foreign companies. With the cost of running their China operation considerably higher now than just a few years ago, home offices are now focused on bottom-line results. Today, it is no longer good enough to just have a presence in China. Companies expect to be profitable, and as quickly as possible. The question headquarters is now asking their mainland operations is, "when are you going to make money?!?"

Keeping Costs Down

As the size of operations in China has grown, and rents and other costs have increased, multinationals know they must conduct their business here more affordably. They are taking a much more critical look at their cost structure and spending. For many, it has become clearly apparent that general and administration costs (G&A) are way out of line with revenue growth. As a result, managing staffing costs has become a key to operating profitably. Among the greatest areas of spending to be reduced is expatriate employees.

Lack Of Qualified Professionals

With the significant changes that have occurred in recent years within China's business environment, it is easy to see why professional manpower demands are far outpacing the supply, particularly for multinational firms. The attention of many industries towards China, the inflow of new companies, and maturing business practices being used by multinationals operating in China has resulted in an overwhelming need for new business skills and expertise that are not yet produced in sufficient numbers locally.

Over the next few years, the search for the right combination of capabilities will become even more critical. Mainly, after years of difficult negotiations and delays, recent breakthroughs now project that China's entry into WTO will happen by the end of 2001. This will have an enormous impact on the open competitiveness of the mainland's domestic industries, ranging from telecom to banking to insurance to consumer products. Although nobody knows which companies will emerge as the biggest winners in China, one thing is certain. The demand for bilingual, international-caliber professionals will further explode as companies look to hire the best talent to compete.

Chapter 4   The Problem: Shortage of Bilingual/ Bicultural Professional Talent

While speaking to an audience of mainland Chinese MBAs recently, a student raised his hand to ask, "what industries would you recommend developing a career in?" My response to him was that it didn't matter which industry he chose. During this period of time, any one is in need of greater numbers of qualified professionals and managers.

Graham Brandt sees China as his company's next billion dollar market. Graham is the former managing director of Microsoft's information technology consulting services in Greater China. He is currently the general manager of Microsoft Hong Kong. However, like many executives who sense the enormous opportunity before them, he sees a difficult problem. "It's not the market in China that's the limiting factor for our growth," he says. "It's finding the right staff with the combination of business development, people, and management skills who can deliver service and customer satisfaction. You don't come across those type often enough here."

It hardly matters what industry you speak of. The situation is the same. They are all short of managers and staff who can conduct business at a high professional standard in China. "Show me any excellent candidates you've got" or "I could have hired him yesterday" are the mantra-like requests we constantly hear from our multinational clients. I've encountered many situations where a job listing remained open for months because a candidate

"It's not the market in China that's the limiting factor for our growth. It's finding the right staff with the combination of business development, people, and management skills who can deliver service and customer satisfaction."

with the appropriate caliber of professional skills and experience simply could not be found.

For expanding multinationals, identifying and hiring top quality personnel with the mix of skills that they need is a key factor in their ability to compete in China. In many cases, companies have had little choice but to transfer out expatriates from their overseas offices. It's expensive and these expatriates usually lack the local experience and capabilities to obtain the results sought. But for many key positions, companies must do so to keep their business in China moving forward until a better option arises.

More Managers Please

Today, foreign expatriates still occupy most of the very top positions within multinational firms. The reasons for this relate to trust, stability, and an understanding of a company's corporate and management objectives.

Instead, the greatest staffing demands are for first and second tier management, at the manager and director levels. The critical need is for well-trained managers who can oversee day-to-day operations, handle key business development functions, and deliver service to clients and customers. They must also have the professional maturity to communicate effectively with senior management, develop and lead staff, and plan strategically.

Expats Need Not Apply

In the past, multinationals regularly transferred expatriates, or expats, to China from their overseas headquarter. Usually, home offices sent managers whose primary value was their knowledge of the company's business, corporate culture, and products. The emphasis was in choosing someone known by headquarters who could keep them abreast of developments in China. Selection was based on a person's achievements abroad. Chinese language skills, market knowledge, and cultural understanding were of little consideration.

In addition, an assignment in China was considered an unattractive proposition, or a hardship posting. It was usually headquarters proposing the transfer, rather than the individual making the request. To entice people, companies offered extremely attractive expat packages to those willing to relocate. Packages could easily double or more the amount of a person's home country compensation. On top of base salary, other premium benefits usually include housing allowance, cost of living adjustment, return trips home, club memberships, and educational allowance for kids. As you can imagine, it's an incredibly expensive way to run a business. Yet, multinationals were doing it this way for years. Time and time again, however, the expat approach has not proven to be an ideal solution for multinationals in China.

With companies focused on keeping costs down these days, expats at all levels are a dying breed. Many stand out like a beacon of light as overpaid hires relative to other talent that could be employed. Language skills and local business capabilities now outweigh the relationship advantages that an expat from home office brings out. As a result, their value placed against their pay package is increasingly difficult to justify.

Today, the hiring strategy for every multinational is the same. Whenever we're briefed on a job opening to be filled, at some point the client inevitably emphasizes that "this is not an expat position." What they want are staff with the level of professional expertise and functional skills they require, but who are also locally qualified and affordable.

It's The Chinese/Western Combination That Counts

Compared to even a few years ago, multinationals are much more experienced and mature with regard to what it takes to do business successfully in China. There is too much at stake not to be smarter in their approach and execution. They have learned that merely using a western way of doing business will not produce the desired results. Rather, to succeed they need staff who can couple international-caliber business practices with an understanding of how to operate effectively in the mainland. Across all industries, this has significantly narrowed the pool of professional and management talent that multinationals wish to employ.

In many ways, China's business environment continues to evolve into a mix of the best of two worlds, East and West. Increasingly, doing business in China is encompassing a broad spectrum of scenarios, from the very Chinese to the very western, and everything in between. As a result, bilingual, international-oriented professionals who are able to handle such a range of situations are finding themselves with a distinct competitive advantage. This is the profile group that is able to realize the best career opportunities within multinational firms in China today.

Chapter 5 A Current Solution: Mainland-born Returnee, Third-country National, and Overseas Chinese Professionals

WHile non-Chinese expatriates from abroad are becoming a less and less desirable solution by multinationals for staffing management ranks in China, a supply of international-caliber talent is seen through the many bilingual Chinese who are educated and trained overseas. These Mainland-born returnee (MBRs), third-country national (from Hong Kong, Taiwan, Singapore, etc.), and overseas Chinese professionals have establish themselves as a *new foreign presence* in China. They possess a different profile and motivation from their non-Chinese, expat predecessors of five to ten years ago. Beyond just having the international business skills and industry expertise sought, they also offer Chinese language and cultural backgrounds, as well as affordability and greater stability for remaining in China.

Many of these Chinese professionals are in their 20s and 30s. They are typically mobile (single or married, without children) and do not necessarily seek expatriate compensation terms as a requirement for relocating to China. Instead, they take a longer term view of the career and financial benefits that working in China can bring. They take stock in their dual cultural and language abilities. Fundamentally, they believe that China is where they can best apply both their Chinese background and international training, and where their greatest opportunities to perform lie.

"The value of overseas Chinese and returnees is clear," points out a human resources director of a major U.S. consumer products company in Shanghai. "Many have the combination of cultural and language skills, international training, and ability to adapt to the mainland's business environment that we need."

"The value of overseas Chinese and returnees is clear. Many have the combination of cultural and language skills, international training, and ability to adapt to the mainland's business environment that we need. "

The category of returnee, third-country national, and overseas Chinese professionals is quite broad in itself. The best suited ones are those who have lived abroad, beginning as teenagers or older. Their Chinese language skills are native, including reading and writing abilities. Having grown up in Asia, they understand Chinese culture, relationships, and practices. They return to visit regularly and have family ties here. This makes them a stable group with regard to their longevity and career focus in Asia. Prime candidates are practically "transparent" from both an Asian and western standpoint. To local Chinese, they are viewed as Chinese. To westerners, they are considered westerners.

Many in this category have gone overseas to attend college or graduate school. Their stays abroad are usually just a few years. The most outstanding quality that makes them attractive to multinational firms in China is whether they've had international work experience within a reputable company. For instance, my firm receives many resumes from Chinese professionals with outstanding academic qualifications from abroad. Unfortunately, they have little or no business experience within a professional environment. For many, the extent of their overseas work experience is in computer centers, research labs, or retail stores. In the past, their connections in China were an attention-getting selling point to multinational companies. However, times have changed. Without the work experience in a recognized company, or an MBA from a leading business school program, they still tend to lack the caliber of professional training sought by multinationals.

In addition, there are those who have moved abroad at a young age. As a result, their personalities and orientation are distinctly westernized. Their spoken Chinese language skills are weak, with many possessing poor reading and writing abilities. Although they may return to Asia occasionally, their exposure to Chinese culture and society is limited.

Though they have the strong educational background and type of professional training that multinationals like, their attractiveness depends on whether they have the bilingual, bicultural backgrounds to operate effectively in China. If they don't, or unless they can offer some highly value-added skill or expertise, then their overwhelmingly westernized backgrounds offer them little long-term competitiveness in the mainland's job market.

No Magic Pill

Although returnees, third-country nationals, and overseas Chinese occupy many management positions within multinationals in China today, there is no "magic pill" or ideal choice regarding which type is considered to be the best to hire. Everyone I've been talked to has their own opinion regarding the effectiveness and value of each group. For instance, although their cultural background, business style, and language skills are well-suited for China, some feel that Taiwanese can be antagonistic and may even look down on the mainland staff they manage. Others feel that Singaporeans and Hong Kongers are out of touch with Chinese culture and are also arrogant towards mainland staff. Chinese from the North America, Europe, and Australia can be too westernized and can lack language abilities that are strong enough to be effective. Even mainland returnees have their weaknesses, as many are often criticized for coming across as feeling superior to colleagues who have not gone abroad. For most companies, the source of professional talent makes little difference. What counts most when doing business in China is one's ability to perform and get results.

Chapter 6 The Ideal Solution: Mainland Professionals With "The Right Stuff"

The Move Towards Localization

Rather than Chinese professionals from abroad, the ideal staffing solution for multinationals in China today is to hire and promote "home-grown" talent. The overwhelming trend is to "localize" operations with mainland professionals who have the caliber and mix of business skills that will allow companies to maintain their professional standards of performance. This is creating excellent opportunities for mainlanders with the "right stuff," or combination of East and West capabilities. In most hiring cases, companies even tell us without hesitation that the person that they're looking for must be a local mainland Chinese.

Affordability

The practical reasons why multinational firms wish to identify and develop local mainland staff are obvious. Perhaps most notable is their lower, less complicated cost relative to foreign hires. For most expatriates new to China, or who have been away for many years, living and working in China is viewed as a hardship. That's why multinationals traditionally add a 15-30% premium on top of base salary, plus housing, recreational, and travel benefits for managers who are transferred to the mainland for assignment.

"In our company, the average director level expatriate costs about US$250,000, " says a regional human resources director for a U.S. telecommunications multinational. "Senior level expats can run close to US$500,000. Some companies out here employ dozens of expats. That's a frightening amount of expense for an operation to carry!"

Real China Hands

There is also a great deal of hand holding that usually takes place to ensure that an expatriate will feel comfortable in their new environment. This takes up a lot of a company's energy and resources. In many cases, despite the extra attention, a person just never adjusts or fits in. Even for those who are able to adapt, it is expected to take a full year on average just for them to figure out how to get things done here. That's a long learning curve in a business environment that is quickly and constantly evolving.

On the other hand, mainland professionals are operating in their "backyard." There is no hardship issue. No special or preferential treatment is required. And there is no adjustment period or risk that the employee will not adapt to their surroundings. Foreigners use the term "China-hand" to describe those expatriates who have worked in the mainland for several years. But essentially, every mainland professional is already a China-hand.

Beyond A Two Year Stint

Mainland hires also offer greater continuity and longevity as employees. Foreign expatriates typically stay for a two to four-year assignment before returning home. In the past, companies accepted this natural turnover as a reality for doing business in the mainland. Today, however, multinationals seek greater stability for their China operations. It's disrupting to have staff leave every couple of years or so, usually at the point when they are just beginning to make real contributions in their jobs. Instead of having an experienced staff in place, another person who is new to China must be trained up again. Continually training and replacing senior managers is a costly, time consuming way to run a business.

Insider Status

"I don't care how long a foreigner has been working in China, there is no way that the quality and extent of their media relationships can match mine." This is what one Beijing manager told me, who has worked six years for a multinational public relations agency. It's difficult for any foreigner to beat the local relationships of a native mainlander who has access to family, alumni, and personal networks. Such relationships often make the difference in whether an objective is achieved, or not.

"I don't care how long a foreigner has been working in China, there is no way that the quality and extent of their media relationships can match mine."

It is no surprise that local mainlanders offer many advantages over foreign expatriates. Yet, the qualifications of most fall short in the eyes of multinationals that have a clear preference to staff their management ranks with more local Chinese professionals. What is missing?

Chapter 7　The Gap:
Ready and Willing,
But Lacking The "Polish"

The scenario appears straightforward enough. On one side, you have expanding multinationals hungry to hire and promote mainland professionals. On the other side you have a large pool of smart, motivated local Chinese talent eager to find excellent job opportunities. But despite such a seemingly ideal matchmaking situation, why do so many mainland professionals face the frustration of not being able to attain job opportunities in leading multinational companies? And if they do, why can't more reach higher management levels?

Local Education System
Test For Success
Unfortunately, despite a deep pool of intellectual talent to draw from, China's education system is not yet nurturing enough of the professional capabilities sought by multinationals. With many more students than top educational programs, whether a young person moves on to the next school level depends on how well they do on a single, rigorous measurement criteria: their national exam scores. For instance, according to statistics from 1998, each year in China there are 1.55 million primary school graduates, 7.04 million junior school graduates, and 1.17 million senior school graduates who cannot enter higher level schools for further study.

Staying Within The Lines
The highly competitive nature of China's education system also has a significant affect on the learning experience students receive. With intense pressure to score well on exams, learning is highly focused on the rote memorization of information. Successful students complete assignments according to instructions. Many tend to be content to follow the rules. In addition, the expectation is often that the professor will distinguish for them what is right and what is wrong. As a result, the creative thinking and problem solving skills that are valued by multinational companies are not very strong.

In contrast, western education systems use more open learning approaches that help develop stronger analytical and decision making skills. Gefei Li is the deputy general manager for Sonoco, a U.S. packaging products and solutions company that services worldwide industrial and consumer customers in 85 countries. Gefei is in charge of sales and marketing, finance, information systems, and supply chain management functions for Sonoco's business ventures in China. When he first started his MBA program at Wake Forrest University in the U.S. in 1991, Gefei recalls how he would diligently prepare calculations before his accounting class. In reviewing homework assignments the next day, the professor would never specify the solution to the problems that were assigned. At some point in every class, Gefei would raise his hand and ask, "so what is the right answer?" The professor would respond by asking him, "what do you think is the right answer?" Then he'd turn to another student and ask the same question.

"At first, I was angry. I thought, this guy is totally irresponsible," recalls Gefei. "I came for answers and he was giving me questions. I was incredibly frustrated because I felt that the professor was wasting my hard-earned money. After a few weeks, however, I began to realize that in the real business world there is not going to be anyone there to tell you what is the right or wrong answer. Sometimes the choice will be between a good solution and very good solution, or a mediocre and bad one. As a manager, you need to be able to analyze situations and make good judgments. That's what the professor was trying to nurture in his class."

"I began to realize that in the real business world there is not going to be anyone there to tell you what is the right or wrong answer. Sometimes the choice will be between a good solution and very good solution, or a mediocre and bad one."

Gene Dorris runs a training company in Shanghai that has worked with thousands of mainland professionals. Aside from creativity and resourcefulness, he feels that the intuition of mainlanders is also not developed to the degree that it should be. "The educational experience of most mainland professionals binds them to the task and the result, with much less emphasis placed on the process," he has observed. "Many would much rather follow orders, than be asked to determine how they should approach a situation themselves."

Regional MBA Programs
Not There Yet

You may wonder to what extent China's graduate business schools are now supplying professionals with the management skills and industry expertise that multinationals seek. Unfortunately, a look at the country's top MBA programs indicate that it may still be a while before China produces enough finance professionals, consultants, marketing managers, business strategists, and other functional specialists with world-class business training.

In its May 2000 issue, *Asiaweek*, a leading regional English-language business magazine, published its first-ever rankings of Asia's MBA programs that listed the region's top 50 business schools. The article ranked Asian MBA programs primarily on their ability to provide students with practical business skills to manage a company and advance their careers, as opposed to their ability to produce thinkers overloaded with management theories.

A look at the list reveals that, of the top 50 full-time programs, only two from China made the list. Only one was actually located on the mainland. That was the China Europe International Business School in Shanghai (a.k.a. the CEIBS program). The other was the Chinese University of Hong Kong. The enrollments of these programs amounted to about 80 and 70 students per year, respectively. In comparison, the Wharton School of Business alone graduates about 800 MBA students each year.

In addition to the smaller number of graduates, the training of these mainland MBAs fell below the standards sought by multinationals. In measuring the quality of these programs on a scale of 1 to 5, where a 5 rating represents a world class level, the *Asiaweek* article rated the CEIBS program and the Chinese University of Hong Kong only 2.81 and 2.84, respectively. A rating of 3 means "outstanding in its country", but not outstanding by international standards.

One Hong Kong-based human resources manager of a major international bank arrived in Shanghai to recruit at a top MBA program. She expected to meet candidates of a similar quality as the ones she met at leading U.S. business schools. Many of the students she interviewed, however, had little or poor caliber work experience prior to entering their program. As a result, they were younger and less polished than their U.S. counterparts who possessed greater previous work experience. After meeting several candidates, she discontinued her recruiting efforts. The professional and international scope she saw simply did not fulfill her bank's requirements.

This is not to say that many of China's professionals will not come from mainland business schools in the future. MBA programs in China are quickly multiplying and are becoming a practical business training option for many local professionals. In addition, these programs are committed to improving, and are doing so rapidly. They are learning from established western programs, through student and faculty exchanges. It will take some more time, however, before mainland institutions produce the caliber of managers in the numbers sought by multinational employers.

The Knowledge and Exposure Gap

Whenever I meet with hiring managers and human resources personnel, the first thing they always emphasize is their company's commitment to localization. They'll go down the list of reasons why they are committed to this objective. Inevitably, however, the conversation always turns to how difficult the result is to actually achieve. The reality is, it is going to take a little more time for mainland staff to mature into the management roles that companies would like them to assume.

One company I know desperately needed a marketing communications manager to cover China. The candidate had to have local media contacts, marketing and management experience, and a professional public relations and advertising background. The firm began looking to fill the position in February. In June, I happened to hear about the position again. Apparently, they had met several candidates through various sources over the five-month period. However, they found nobody who met the requirements. The position continued to remain open. This is not such an unusual case.

Although the presence of local professionals in management ranks has increased significantly over the past few years, there is still a shortage of mainland professionals with the level of "polish" or "exposure" that multinationals require to fill key positions. This gap, however, is being crossed by many who have managed to attain the skills and capabilities that are being actively sought. The rest of this book focuses mainly on those personal and professional qualities that are most valued in multinational organizations, and what one can do to develop them.

Part III

Getting into a Multinational Firm

Chapter 8 What Are Multinational Managers Looking For?

Professionalism
Initiative
Team Player
Accountability
Leadership
Open-Minded

The young man who approached me after my presentation in Beijing on *Developing A Career In A Multinational Firm* was perplexed. He had listened to me talk about mainland professionals who were attaining exceptional opportunities and doing extremely well in multinational companies. His English was good, and he had several years of work experience with a reputable Chinese company. He kept himself up-to-date with international events and business developments. Yet, he was puzzled over why others with backgrounds seemingly no more qualified than his were able to get into such promising jobs, while he couldn't.

There wasn't a single answer I could give him. However, among those candidates that we work with who have successfully entered and developed a career in a multinational company, some things are common among them. Skills such as English language ability, industry expertise, or management experience are, of course, attractive to any company. But perhaps more importantly, there are key intangible qualities that many multinational managers place even greater value on when evaluating prospective employees. Although the order of importance varies, the following are repeatedly mentioned by executives and human resources personnel whom I have posed the question to: what are the most important characteristics that you look for when hiring new staff and promoting key people?

Highly Sought Employee Characteristics

- *Professionalism*
- *Loyalty and Transparency*
- *Accountability*
- *Effective Communications Skills*
- *Understanding The Big Picture*
- *International-Oriented Thinking*
- *Team Player*
- *Leadership*
- *Initiative*
- *Open-minded*
- *Finding Solutions*
- *Values*
- *The Right Attitude*
- *One Foot In Asia, One Foot In The West*

Professionalism

If there is one word that summarizes the overall qualities that multinationals seek in those they employ and promote, it would be professionalism. The definition of that word, although easy to understand, is much harder to specify. It varies with each executive you ask.

Several multinational managers whom I've spoken with relate professionalism to the quality of the endgame. Meaning, is the result you achieve something that your boss is happy with? Or that the customer is happy with? Frank Chen is the director of marketing in Shanghai for one of the world's largest international fast-moving consumer goods companies. He associates professionalism with performing in a manner where you are "doing more and better than just what the manual says." It's being true to your own internal standard and commitment of how well you know you should perform a task. That is rooted in how much you care, and not just going through the motions of the job you are doing.

"You can see it most clearly in the service industry," says Frank. "In whether the person you are dealing with is doing their best to please you. It's seen in a genuine smile and attitude that shows that they care about being helpful to you. That's something that reaches beyond what you are required to do. It comes from the heart."

Sheridan Yen has been managing information technology software applications and service operations in both Greater China and the United States for over 15 years. Currently, he is the managing director of SUNeVision, the regional technology arm of Sun Hung Kai Properties, based out of Hong Kong. Sheridan attaches professionalism to having a respect for others. He believes that such a fundamental respect reflects on the way one deals with colleagues and customers, and on one's ability to cooperate and respond as a team player.

Susan Pattis is the CEO of a newly formed management consulting firm and service provider called ChinaClicks2 Consulting Company. Over the past 12 years, she has also held senior management roles in leading international companies, such as American Express (charge cards), Edelman (public relations), and AchieveGlobal (training), in both China and the U.S. Susan relates professionalism to a person's openness to outside input. To her, it is demonstrated in a person's willingness to accept and assess feedback from others, as opposed to taking comments personally and reacting emotionally.

In general, each of these definitions of professionalism begins with an understanding of what your responsibilities are to your colleagues, to your management, and to your customers. It is then demonstrated through consistent performance that acts in the best interest of the company and the team you're a part of, rather than just for one's own personal interests.

Each of these definitions of professionalism begins with an understanding of what your responsibilities are to your colleagues, to your management, and to your customers.

Unfortunately, many multinational executives I talk to feel that too many mainland professionals today do not have a strong understanding of what professionalism is. And this hurts their performance and ability to attain better opportunities for themselves. For instance, rather than demonstrating accountability to others, their mentality can often be self-centered. It is too win/lose or yours/mine oriented, where their own gains come at the expense of the organization or other colleagues.

Overall though, Sheridan Yen believes that young mainland professionals today have a lot going for them. He sees China's professional middle class being formed over the next five years. "The caliber of mainland professionals is much higher today, than even 3-4 years ago," observes Sheridan. "Their exposure to international business standards is quite good. Now that ideologies about business and capitalism are evolving, they're ready to move to the next level. The young people of China understand that professionalism, and professional maturity, is the way to a good future. They want to learn and improve. They are open to new things and are willing to take risks, and even fail. When it comes to performing at a high professional standard, increasingly, they are able to talk the talk, and walk the walk."

Loyalty and Transparency

One concern that multinational companies have about mainland staff has to do with their sense of loyalty to the company. They need to assess the priorities of key staff, particularly of those in management roles. For well-run international firms, employees are looked upon as a long-term investment, who will benefit from the company's training, mentoring, and development resources.

With many mainland professionals heavily focused on salary and anxious to advance their career track, however, it is difficult to measure the weight they place on factors such as corporate culture, job satisfaction, and future promotional opportunities. After decades of austere living and scarcity of resources, many older mainlanders do not take a long-term view of their career prospects. Instead, their outlook is oriented around what they can obtain now. Situations such as China's current economic prosperity may not last long. So if an opportunity presents itself, better to seize it now. "It's difficult entrusting your China marketing strategy for a key product or business to someone who may readily jump to your competitor for an additional RMB1,000 a month," points out one multinational executive.

Lack of transparency in the priorities of mainland staff can have an especially large affect on how multinational companies approach their investment in developing high potential employees. For instance, management realizes that to advance into higher management ranks, key mainland staff need greater international exposure, such as chances to visit overseas operations. But their fear is that as soon as they make the investment, their good people will leave soon afterwards. In one example, a client of ours sent twenty operations managers for training in Singapore earlier this year. Within three months of their return, five had already left the company. It's instances like this that cause multinationals to be cautious about investing in training opportunities for their mainland staff.

Developing a successful career in a multinational firm requires more than just a strong knowledge of international business practices. What also counts is your ability to elicit the trust and confidence of senior management and home office. Many Chinese make a clear distinction between their personal and professional life and, as a result, tend not to open themselves up within the office. They remain an unknown entity whose goals and priorities cannot be measured by the company. Greater transparency allows management in multinational companies to develop staff with the commitment and resources it takes to advance them into greater roles of responsibility.

Accountability
Admitting Mistakes

The mentality of many mainlanders is that you can only report good news. When it comes to bad news, Chinese culture shows a tendency to shoot the messenger. Therefore, when many Chinese professionals run up against a problem they can't solve, or are not achieving the results that they are expected to, they suffer by themselves. Their unwillingness to share bad news stops them from asking for help. As a result, management is often the last to know when something is wrong. By that time, the problem has gotten out of hand.

In the U.S., reporting problems is not necessarily bad. Help is sought out more readily. There is a much better understanding among professionals that the ultimate goal is to do whatever is necessary to get the result. Oftentimes, all that is needed to accomplish that is to seek the assistance and support from those who can help you identify a solution or set you in the right direction.

Jeffrey Reed is the former general manager of Best Foods in Beijing, a US$60bn U.S. food company that has been operating in the mainland since 1984. Until his recent return to the U.S., he headed their China operation since 1996. In his experience, he has also found that many mainland professionals try to avoid giving a straight answer, especially when it comes to taking responsibility for something they've done that is not going well. He has seen some staff go to great lengths not to report a problem. They've called in sick, sent others to speak for them, or have even blatantly denied their involvement in a matter. Sometimes, they'll just point the finger elsewhere and say, "he did it, it wasn't me."

"To avoid such a feeling of anxiety in my staff, whenever I began a conversation with one of my line managers, I used a "bnf" approach, or bad news first, ," says Jeffrey. "I'd start a meeting by saying to them, "okay, bnf." I found that it lightened the way a potentially bad situation is communicated and brought it out into the open in a straightforward, less threatening manner. "

Seeking Help

Jeffrey would much rather have his staff tell him that they don't know the answer to a question, than try to wing it. "Many get defensive and emotional, or even start arguing with you whenever they are challenged, rather than try to listen and understand your intention," says Jeffrey. "It shows their insecurity and lack of maturity. I believe it's because they don't truly believe in themselves. They don't feel they are good enough to still be viewed positively if they don't always have the right answer or get the right result."

Although it's natural to not want to take the blame for something, from a multinational manager's perspective, the purpose of pointing out a mistake or failure is usually to correct the problem so it can be avoided in the future. Good managers recognize that there is a learning curve for any new task that someone takes on.

"Sometimes I just want to coach and advise some of my staff, but they take it as criticism," says a sales director for a large U.S. consumer products

"Sometimes I just want to coach and advise some of my staff, but they take it as criticism. They get defensive over simple comments that are clearly meant as feedback."

company. "They get defensive over simple comments that are clearly meant as feedback. As a manager, you only have so much time and energy before you lose interest in trying to help someone and have to move on. It's really to their detriment, since they no longer receive the critical feedback they need to improve. By being more open and trusting, it would increase their overall ability to learn and succeed."

Christine Zhou is a sales manager for a leading international pharmaceutical company. She points to her willingness to seek advice from others as a key success factor in her own career development. Christine will ask for help whenever she faces a problem she knows she can't solve on her own, within the expected timeframe. "My main objective is always to find a solution and get the result. Many mainland Chinese don't recognize that," says Christine. "Instead, they'll spend all their time and energy trying not to fail or trying not to look bad. I've seen colleagues stop in the middle of a project, because they don't know what to do. In the end, they tend not to get as involved. This limits their exposure. When you run up against something you can't solve, you don't always need to be so clever to come up with a solution. Usually, you only need to be smart enough to identify and ask someone who can help you figure out the problem."

Effective Communications skills

As important as any skill, the ability to communicate effectively can affect your ability to manage, get results, and ultimately, succeed in a multinational organization.

Respect Your Boss' Time

When mainland professionals do have something to say, they often lack the effectiveness in getting their point across to senior management. Ideas are given, but never heard from again. Often, it has to do with how the ideas are presented. Many are unfocussed in their presentation of information and ideas. As a result, they end up being too long-winded with what they have to say. Or they have a tendency to go too deep into details, beyond what is appropriate during the initial presentation of an idea. Ultimately, they fail to capture the attention or interest of their senior management.

So what is the best way is to communicate an idea to your boss? To begin with, you should be confident that any good manager will want to hear ideas that can help the company perform better. However, you should also recognize and respect their time pressures and priorities. Busy executives typically juggle many tasks at once.

Their attention span to focus on what you have to say is usually brief. Therefore, you may only have five minutes of their time to get your idea across.

As a result, speak less and think more. The key is to be concise. Most executives are excellent decision-makers. They are also very perceptive. They are able to extract information, identify key points, and make quick assessments on just about everything going on around them. You shouldn't think otherwise, just because they don't tell you or because you can't see it.

Present Ideas From The Top On Down

It is also important to present information to management in an impactful manner. To do this, you should think from the top on down. What that means is that your initial remarks should always focus on the big picture. First see if they are interested in your idea by highlighting the benefits to your company, your customers, your department, or to other employees. For example, when presenting your idea, point out the impact on improved response time to customers. Or if you have a production improvement idea, convey how time, cost, and/or effort can be saved.

Typically, busy managers don't care to be bothered with the details. They want to know the bottom-line benefit to the company. However, once the result or advantage is apparent, if they are interested in knowing more specifics, they'll ask. If they don't, then you don't need to waste your time or theirs going deeper into them.

Clarity Of Thought

Jeffrey Reed ranks clarity of presentation and thought as the characteristic that he values most in his mainland staff. "Whenever I discuss an issue with my staff, I want to see forethought and evidence of understanding and planning," says Jeffrey. "However, many do not always follow a logical, sequential path of reasoning. Their comments jump around, or are inconsistent. Their thought process does not indicate that they've sorted out what is meaningful and relevant. Instead, they'll try to bluff their way through a discussion.

"Beyond just an answer, I want to know how they plan to execute. I want to hear it explained so I can understand the logic in their approach."

It doesn't take long before it becomes apparent

why. It's because they've come unprepared."

Sheridan Yen echoes that opinion. "Beyond just an answer, I want to know how they plan to execute," he emphasizes. "I want to hear it explained so I can understand the logic in their approach. That way I can tell if they really understand the keys issues and what must be done to solve the problem."

Being Direct

Although in Chinese culture it is not considered polite to speak out in a direct manner, in a multinational environment, expressing oneself in a straightforward way is common practice. A worldwide survey by a leading U.S. consumer electronics company showed that among all its international operations, their China employees complained the most. "They are always complaining behind the back of management," says the human resources director. "The worst of it is, management has little idea this is happening, or that there are even any issues of concern among our employees."

"Chinese people are very keqi (polite), to the point of being too much so," says Greg Li, who has spent five years in China doing business in the areas of manufacturing and property development. "You may think that they agree with you or understand what is going on, but it's often the case where the exact opposite is true. As a manager, you want to know what your staff are thinking, so you know if they are in tune with what you are telling them, or if they have concerns. That can only happen if they express themselves in a way that is in line with what's on their mind."

... But Be Sure You Have Good Reason

At the same time, there are some who get into trouble for being too direct. Recently, a mainland candidate I was speaking with revealed that because of his directness with others, he was often accused of being arrogant. Why do some people come across as straightforward and open, while others are seen to be arrogant?

"It all has to do with what your objective is," explains one U.S. executive. "If the reason for your directness is for your own benefit, then people will view it as arrogance. They will sense that you are speaking out just to prove that you are right or show that you are superior, or because it is important for you just to make your point. However, if you are being direct for the benefit of someone else, then they will sense something different. You might have some advice or insight to share that can help a person's situation, or have an idea or valuable feedback to provide them with. People can distinguish between an intent that is meant to be helpful, as opposed to one that is self-serving."

Speak English?

Of course, what affects your ability to communicate effectively the most in a multinational company environment is English language ability. My company specializes in placing bilingual professionals within leading international firms at management levels. For about 90 percent of the job openings we see in China, spoken English (at a business level) is a must, with strong reading and writing abilities highly preferred. These positions usually require candidates to interface often with international managers, as well as communicate updates and information to China-based and home office senior management. Beyond just speaking, candidates must be able to express themselves accurately and clearly.

Janet Tan, former director of Andersen Consulting's Greater China technology consulting practice, places the greatest value on strong English language speakers when hiring new staff, even though most of her team's projects are with mainland clients. "We handle large-scale information systems projects and work with a lot of information and instructions on new technology from the U.S." says Janet. "If someone can't speak English, you introduce a significant uncertainty factor into the equation. You can't be fully confident going through translators. They misinterpret and don't always understand the objectives and nuances of the technology or business discussions. There are enough horror stories of projects and deals that fail because of miscommunication, or because someone was unable to respond clearly in English."

If Not Words, Then Numbers!

Stephen Wood simplifies the language issue with his management team, which is made up entirely of mainlanders. Although most internal meetings are conducted in Chinese, his managers must often communicate in English to the company's U.S. Board of Directors. Stephen tells his managers that he doesn't always need them to give him words. Often, he asks them for numbers instead. "As a parts supplier, numbers are the clearest indicator of results in areas like performance, delivery time, or quantities shipped," explains Stephen. "I can attach the words to the figures, but it's the numbers that tell the story and form the basis of any report to management on whether performance is improving, decreasing, or remaining flat. Our managers are starting to understand the significance of evaluating the numbers, and are now doing their own analysis to identify trends and problem areas."

Meaning Above All Else

More important than strong spoken English skills is the ability to accurately interpret the meaning of what's being said. "After giving instructions or describing a situation to my staff, I find that there are many instances where they just don't get my full meaning," says a Canadian executive for a property development company in Shanghai. "What is said verbally is only 50% of communication. I know they understand the words, but they don't always grasp the intent or meaning. Part of that has to do with the language, but a lot of it has to do with whether or not the person has a broader understanding of international concepts, practices, and perspectives."

Ultimately, to resolve issues and communicate with foreign management, it helps to understand their priorities and why they might think in a certain way. This affects your ability to deliver the right message and respond to situations in the most appropriate manner. "Gaining an understanding of what's important to your management begins with opening your mind and removing your biases and preconceived views about what they think," he continues. "If you can do this at a subconscious level, then you'll be able to better communicate in a way in which foreign managers will respond."

Understanding The Big Picture

International companies in China want their management staff to have a big picture perspective with regards to the priorities of the corporation. Such a perspective is critical to one's ability to direct resources and effort in ways that best fulfill company objectives.

Unfortunately, many mainland professionals do not have the understanding of and exposure to company issues that extend beyond their job function, or that encompass larger industry trends and competitive scenarios. Many are not even aware of what it is they should be seeing. This impacts their ability to meet corporate objectives and inhibits them from being stronger decision-makers and managers. The shortcoming can affect their promotability to higher roles.

For instance, for many mainland professionals it is not a top priority for them to save the company money. "I've seen many situations where a person will spend

$100 of the company's money if it saves $10 that will make them look good," says one multinational executive. "The mentality is to use up the company's resources for themselves. From a senior manager's perspective, this severely limits a person's attractiveness to the organization. I want employees who are not so territorial, but who view things from a perspective that goes beyond just the benefits that they might receive as an individual."

Aligning Benefits

Like many multinational executives, Sheridan Yen feels that mainland professionals need to recognize the importance of aligning their own personal benefits with those of the company. In an international company, such an alignment of benefits gives management greater assurance that an employee will do the right thing when faced with an ambiguous situation. If someone understands that doing the right thing by the company is also good for themselves, then they'll likely make a proper decision when a critical situation arises.

Embracing Change

In Chinese companies, employees tend not to think about change. For many, the objective is to reach a point of comfort and stability. As a result, when business is running smoothly, most mainland staff do not understand why they should challenge things. It relates to their lack of a broader, long-term perspective of a company's objectives and the competitive, dynamic forces of the business environment that it operates in.

Multinationals in China, on the other hand, are always pursuing change. Innovative, initiative, leading-edge, and risk are words that they emphasize and embrace in their corporate culture. For them, change must happen if they are to compete successfully within the mainland's constantly evolving markets. To stay ahead of their competition, they value managers who are forward looking with regards to future opportunities, as well as to new and better ways of doing business.

Do Anything

To help acquire a big picture perspective, Susan Pattis encourages her staff to do anything that will expand their mind. "I tell them to enlarge their social circles and get to know professionals from other functional areas and industries," says Susan. "Or to read a book, take a class, or just have conversations with colleagues and friends about things of interest. They can all help you gain greater insight and recognize new approaches to the daily situations you face at work. Most importantly, it develops your ability to deal with different people and to solve problems from different angles."

International-Oriented Thinking

Where English language abilities were once a ticket for getting a job, today they are merely a baseline requirement for entering a multinational company. To progress up the management ranks though, one must possess a mature, professional way of doing things. Such a standard of thinking and performance are best gained through exposure to leading international business practices. For managers in a multinational firm, it is important to have insight into the situations you encounter and into what is most important to those you are dealing with in your company. As a result, multinationals favor candidates with work experience from reputable international companies. Such experience significantly reduce a candidate's learning curve and make for a smoother transition into a multinational's operation and business approach.

For managers in a multinational firm, it is important to have insight into the situations you encounter and into what is most important to those you are dealing with in your company.

It is not absolutely necessary, however, for staff to have worked abroad or with an international company previously. Most critical is that your experience has been developed within a high caliber, professional environment. For instance, you may have worked before in a small Chinese company, but the manager who supervised you worked previously with a leading multinational firm. As a result, the professional training you have received is of an exceptional standard.

The reverse can also be true. Many well-educated mainland professionals have been exposed to international environments and business concepts, but still lack professional skills that are considered genuinely strong. They think much bigger of themselves than how other people see them. It's because most of their international training has been attained through undergraduate or graduate courses. Their English is learned in classrooms and knowledge of leading business practices through articles and books. Based on these experiences, they believe they hold an advantage for getting a job and succeeding in a multinational firm. Yet, in reality they have faced few situations where these concepts have been put into practice, or have interacted with few professionals who regularly demonstrate business capabilities of a high caliber. Unfortunately, such peripheral exposure does not attract the attention today that one might anticipate, or provide the skills that one should have.

For successful professionals, real learning happens in the workplace, by working with and observing others who are stronger and more experienced than you are professionally. If your training is without depth and your abilities are not of a high international standard, then you need to evaluate your attractiveness to multinational firms. This doesn't mean you have to give up on your goal of working in a top company. You just have to continue to work hard at attaining the skills you need and objectives you seek. Many success stories of mainland professionals show that it can be done. However, it will take a commitment and dedicated effort to make happen.

Team Player

For Sheridan Yen, a person's ability to be a strong team player is among the most important qualities that he seeks when hiring new staff. Unfortunately, it is said that Chinese people prefer to be the head of a chicken, than the tail of a cow. The saying does not reflect well on the ability of mainland professionals to perform well as team players.

The Concept Of Win/Win

The concept of a win/win situation is not an engrained one for many mainlanders whose approach to situations is oriented around competing, and not teamwork. Perhaps it comes from an attitude from early on that you have to be the best. Or because Chinese people are used to an environment based on scarcity, rather than abundance. As a result, many are unwilling to share what is considered valuable, such as knowledge or expertise. For an organization, the undesirable result is too much competition among staff, who end up fighting among themselves for opportunities and leadership roles.

"Among Chinese people, it is said that usually only a maximum of three people can get along," says Sheridan. "In actuality, two is more often the case. Team mentality is typically weak among mainland staff that I've managed. Middle managers tend to have a strong cultural imprint of mistrust in each other. I've seen many who don't want to work for other local mainland managers. Others are reluctant to transfer their knowledge and skills to colleagues. Or, they'll turn against the next person just to protect themselves. But if you expect to move up in a multinational organization, you have to be able to work across different groups and departments."

Supporting Other Departments

It's not so hard to build a team from a fixed group, according to Nandani Lynton. Nandani is the CEO of a human resources consulting company in Beijing called Haarmann Hemmelrath Management Consultants, that has worked on many organizational behavior consulting projects for corporate clients. "In my experience, mainland professionals perform well in teams where staff come from the same department and have a chance to work closely together and become familiar with each other" explains Nandani. "Trust and credibility are built over time, and a tight group or "family" can be formed. However, building cross-functional teams where mainlanders are not part of the same family and where they must cooperate on projects together is a different story. While communication happens upward and downward, they do not occur across. Situations are created where the feeling is "your boss is not my boss, why should I help you or listen to what you say." Mainland managers need to trust and support each other more. By sharing information and resources, they'll grow much faster and more effectively in their organization."

Leadership

One of the biggest challenges Sheridan faces when building an organization in China is identifying strong first and second line managers (i.e. those who supervise staff). "Most mainland professionals lack strong management skills," says Sheridan. "They either possess the good guy syndrome, where they try to be a person who is well liked, but don't take a stand on anything. Instead, they act only as a messenger through which to communicate directives. Or, they are the military type, where they take an autocratic, authoritarian approach to managing staff. Communication for them is one directional, downward."

Force Of Personality, Rather Than Authority

For multinational senior managers like Sheridan, they are not looking for staff who stand out as a star in the company, but for ones who can work with and help those around them to succeed. "Most Chinese people associate leadership with authority, particularly in SOEs," Sheridan continues. "That's not the case in an international organization, where leadership stems from your presence, or force of personality. That is expressed through your maturity, genuine confidence, interest in other people, and concern for the team. What is valued is an ability to build the kind of trust and loyalty among your staff and other internal departments. That ultimately allows you to work out issues and get results."

> *"Most Chinese people associate leadership with authority, particularly in SOEs. That's not the case in an international organization, where leadership stems from your presence, or force of personality."*

More Than Just Delegating Responsibility

Many mainlanders look at a management role as an opportunity to delegate responsibility and to reduce their own workload. However, it is more than just being given decision-making authority. Rather, your primary role as a manager is to support and develop the people under you so they can succeed. Although providing for the development needs of others sounds easy enough to do, it can be quite difficult, particularly for first time managers whose early success has been built on being a strong individual contributor. Instead of focussing on themselves, they must now put the well-being and benefit of others before their own.

Reluctance To Train Others

In China, where so much emphasis is placed on position and hierarchies, getting promoted to a management level in a multinational company is seen as a significant achievement. After getting there, however, many are afraid to jeopardize or lose the position they've achieved. As a result, many Chinese managers don't view teaching others as beneficial to their own situation. The willingness to share information with and assist colleagues is not commonplace. It is only seen as creating a threat for themselves.

In international organizations, the mentality is the exact opposite. Western managers understand that developing subordinates is a fundamental way in which to advance your career. They recognize that it is to their advantage to obsolete themselves from their current job. That means training somebody who can eventually take over their position. "A lot of my time is spent on managing and developing my direct reports," says Ying Han, Chief Financial Officer of AsiaInfo Technologies. "The better I do this, the more it frees up my time to think about and get involved in higher level issues and achievements."

Those who are able to raise the performance and success of others are able to prove their management capabilities and potential for higher levels of responsibility in the company. To senior management in multinationals, developing and ensuring the success of staff is an important indication of one's leadership skills, as well as maturity and understanding of what is most beneficial for the organization.

Initiative

Too Passive

Like many multinational executives, Frank Chen looks for initiative and entrepreneurial drive within his top staff. He defines this as a willingness to take ownership of whatever task is at hand, and not just collecting a paycheck or doing what the job description says.

However, in many of his mainland staff, he senses a desire to only seek a secure job. They are more than happy to just be holding a position in an international company. They play it safe by going through the motions of what they are asked to do, and little more. Rather than think even, they prefer to be instructed and just asked to execute. What Frank wants to see though is staff who really drive for results. He refers to that drive by another term, passion.

When it comes to taking initiative, many mainlanders are hesitant. They have been trained in much of their upbringing to be order takers. Or, they are afraid to lose the opportunity they've gained. It stems from a mentality that those who make too much noise will be punished, like the fattest pig is the one that will be slaughtered first. Others are in the habit of delegating upward and passing on problems to their superiors. "They view themselves as just lowly subordinates," says Frank. "They take an attitude that you're the boss, and the one earning the big money. Therefore, it's your responsibility to solve the problem. Or, they position themselves at an inferior level, relative to the foreign managers, and are unwilling to take on greater tasks or voice their opinions.

Speak Up

As a result, many mainland professionals are not outspoken enough when it comes to communicating their concerns and ideas to management. Ron Chow works as a sales manager for a U.S. business equipment manufacturer in Beijing. When he first joined his company in 1994, he noticed that he was always participating the least during

"Because I rarely spoke up, I found out later that nobody thought I knew what was going on."

management meetings attended by foreign managers. "Because I rarely spoke up, I found out later that nobody thought I knew what was going on." he recalls. "It's not my habit to shine like a bulb, so I rarely expressed my opinions, even though I often had ideas that I felt were good. Instead, I'd approach others one on one, outside of the meetings. It was very time consuming though. Eventually, I realized that I was missing the opportunities to contribute during the critical time when decisions were being made, which was in the meetings."

Another mainland manager in Shanghai also found it difficult initially to adjust to the business style of the U.S. software company he worked for. "Our foreign managers were introducing a lot of new business concepts to the Chinese management team," he explains. "Many of the ideas were good, but some were not appropriate for the way business is done in China. Because the other Chinese managers and I were not as vocal and willing to debate issues, it ended up taking our company a long time to determine the best approach for our business here. A lot of time was wasted going in a direction that many of us knew was not optimal to begin with."

Frank Chen wishes more of his staff would speak up in meetings, whether in Chinese or English. In determining their management potential, he evaluates people not simply on what they do, but on how they express themselves. "I don't need notetakers," says Frank. "What I want to hear is a point of view, any point of view. If they expect to be given greater responsibility, mainland professionals need to first ask themselves if they can challenge authority. My really good staff have the maturity and confidence to disagree with me and put forth their own ideas. I just love that."

Saying No

"Mainland professionals also have to learn to say no, when it is called for. Sometimes, you just have to challenge you managers," says Jackie He, a senior manager for business planning and strategic development for a telecommunications equipment manufacturer in Beijing. "Senior management does not always know what is happening at the lower levels. As a result, they do not always make decisions that are best for a particular department or group. Without being more vocal, a good deal of time and effort can be wasted"

Jackie gives one example of her regional headquarter's sudden request for information, in which a response was expected within a few days. The information, however, normally took weeks to compile. Instead of just responding immediately to the request, Jackie thought it better for all parties involved to explain to headquarters what it would take to pull together the information. She also wanted to confirm if the information was absolutely necessary in the time frame that was given, or even if it was worth putting together at all, given the effort it would require. Upon hearing Jackie's assessment of the project, headquarters relaxed their deadline for the request. As a result, her department was able to avoid the disruption, while still meeting the needs of the regional office.

Take Responsibility

Overall, international companies and their management support and value those who are willing to assume responsibility. But it's not always the case where someone will tell you exactly where the boundaries are. "I always tell my staff, that if you believe you have a good reason to make a judgment, then please do," says Michael Chu, director at a leading international public relations firm in Beijing. "The most important thing is to think a situation or problem through. Consider the risk and the potential. If you're always looking for someone else to make the decisions for you and you don't take any responsibility or authority upon yourself, then you're not growing as a professional. From my standpoint, even if one of my staff makes a mistake, I'm willing to bear the loss for the experience that is gained, as long as the person's actions are based on a reasonable assessment of the situation."

"Even if one of my staff makes a mistake, I'm willing to bear the loss for the experience that is gained, as long as the person's actions are based on a reasonable assessment of the situation."

Open-Minded
... And An Ability To Learn

For multinational doing business in mainland, identifying staff with the ability to train and learn fast is crucial. "Everything we are doing in China is new, evolving, or being learned as we go," says a project manager for a systems integration solutions multinational in Shanghai. "That includes the markets we target, as well as the professional business practices and expertise that we must demonstrate to our customers. To get up to speed, and then to keep up with the new situations that are constantly happening, our people need to be highly trainable. Fundamentally, that requires a strong desire to learn and an open-mind."

Many multinational managers will even avoid looking at candidates with backgrounds that indicate that they came from a conservative or traditional environment. With company cultures that are aggressive and demand a high level of performance, their concern is that it will be too difficult or take too long for these candidates to change their way of thinking. "We know that many new staff who join us won't yet have the knowledge and skills to perform at the level that is expected of them. But they need to get there quickly," continues the project manager. "Our company adheres pretty strictly to the probation period objectives that they expect new hires to achieve. We'll teach them what they need to know to be successful. But the ones who make it are the ones who show flexibility in their thinking and, therefore, have an ability to absorb new concepts and to take on new approaches to doing things."

Sheridan Yen ties trainability directly to his most important hiring criteria. Along with integrity, he identifies the ability to learn as the top two qualities that he looks for in the prospective mainland staff that he hires. "If I can find just these two things in a candidate, I'll hire them on the spot!" he exclaims.

Finding solutions
Thinking Outside The Box

For multinational companies that are continually introducing new products and services into new markets, doing business in China is like driving someplace you've never been to without a road map. There are no directions to guide you and few people to tell you how to get to where you want to go. As a result, multinational clients are always asking us to introduce candidates to them who can approach business situations creatively and resourcefully. Because there is usually no existing precedence to follow, they need staff with strong problem solving abilities, ones who can think outside the box. Unfortunately, these qualities are not especially strong among many mainland professionals.

"I find that Chinese professionals are very good at observing," says Chi Wei Wang, a director at Anderson Consulting in Beijing. "They can identify problems and talk at length about them. When it comes to analyzing the problems and offering solutions though, they tend to be much weaker. I've had countless encounters where my staff will spend a great deal of effort summarizing a scenario or problem that we're trying to solve. Eventually, they end up just repeating to me exactly what I've told them in the first place. That's not what I need. What I need is for them to tell me what can be done to solve the problem."

Being Resourceful

Gefei Li recalls one highly-qualified candidate he hired from a leading international fast-moving consumer goods manufacturer. On paper, his credentials appeared right. He was a smart guy, who was quite successful in his earlier company. Yet, he failed miserably in his new position. "This guy came to our company blinded by the business approach of his previous company, which was very process oriented and structured," recalls Gefei. "Unfortunately, he couldn't do things any other way. There was no flexibility in his thinking. In the end, it was apparent that he just didn't have a street smart approach to facing the type of obstacles that are encountered in our business. He knew how to fit into a corporate role, but lacked an "own the business" mentality and resourcefulness that is needed to get results in more unpredictable situations."

Helen Qi is a sales manager in Beijing for one of the world's leading international electronic business news services. Helen always tries to look at the positive side of any situation. "When my company first began promoting our news service in the mainland, Chinese clients resisted because we only offered the service in English," describes Helen. "They would tell me that they preferred that the news be in Chinese, which is what all our competitors offered."

"Rather than just accept their existing viewpoint, what I told them was that WTO was just around the corner. And to think of how much time their employees spend studying from English books, and the emphasis their company is always placing on staff to improve their English capabilities. By buying our news service, it would help their employees develop greater English capabilities and ultimately help their organization reach its objective of developing into an international company. By sharing with our clients this perspective, we've been able to successfully sell our English services into many Chinese companies."

Always Ask Questions

The key to finding good solutions is to first ask good questions. "In too many situations, our mainland staff just take things for granted or just believe what they are told," according to an executive in Shanghai. "They'll read or hear something, but don't look deeper to question the degree to which it might be true, the perspective or source that it comes from, or the logic of the information. Of course, it's important to think outside the box in order to come up with creative solutions. But you have to begin by first asking more questions inside the box."

Values
Cherish Who You Are

During my many interviews for this book, a surprising, yet often repeated characteristic was identified as one that many executives felt too many young professionals lacked enough of today. It went beyond qualities such as initiative, resourcefulness, or effective communication skills. Rather, the characteristic that was often mentioned was the attention to personal values.

For Gefei Li, strong values are the first thing he looks for when considering a new staff member for his team. His definition of this characteristic is understanding and appreciating who you are and where you've come from, knowing how to conduct yourself properly, and having a sense of what is most important in life. Gefei is able to spot these things in those who display a humbleness, open-mind, down-to-earth personality, and willingness to work hard. They are qualities he believes are fundamental to any person's success as a professional. As a result, his best advice to young professionals is to try to identify

A humbleness, open mind, down-to-earth personality, and willingness to work hard. They are qualities he believes are fundamental to one's success as a professional.

and understand the values they cherish. "Those who do this well usually possess an integrity and "solidness of character" that others are able to see and that is highly attractive to multinational managers like myself," says Gefei.

Unfortunately, rather than basing important career decisions on personal values, Gefei sees too many young mainlanders pursuing things and making key career moves based on the wrong reasons, and without a real understanding of why. For instance, they place too much belief on education and credentials. Once they have acquired them, they think they are entitled to receiving good jobs, promotions, and financial rewards. Although they may attain such opportunities in the short-term, they sacrifice sound fundamentals and overlook the work ethic of building something solid from the ground up that will eventually lead to greater, long-term career success.

Caring for Others

Susan Pattis is even more direct in how she sees young Chinese professionals today. "So many I meet appear lost," she says frankly. "Although the academic training and basic skills that today's younger generation receives is quite good, too much emphasis is placed on class ranking and grades. On top of this, the society is placing an increasingly greater weight on making money and being successful. On the other hand, there is little guidance being offered about life. Too few parties are emphasizing how to be a good person and the need to take responsibility for others. Those things are very important when working for a multinational organization, where career success relies on your ability to be a strong team player, and to do what's right for your colleagues and the company. Ultimately, it is your interest in caring about others that defines your professionalism and potential as a leader."

Beyond the application of strong personal qualities towards one's overall success in a multinational company, Susan also emphasizes their importance towards being a good manager as well. "I don't believe someone can be an effective manager without first being a real person themselves. It's important to have good academic qualifications, but it's also necessary to understand

"I don't believe someone can be an effective manager without first being a real person themselves. It's important to have good academic qualifications, but it's also necessary to understand what is important in the lives of others."

what is important in the lives of others. To manage well, you need to know what are the motivations, desires, and concerns of the people around you. Like being a good person, being a good manager does not happen overnight. It's a lifelong pursuit."

Similar to Gefei, Susan advises her staff to be in tune with and to appreciate their own personal experience, and not just to follow what the media and outside world is hyping. She also places a great deal of emphasis on cherishing values and being comfortable with your own identity. Finally, she believes in the long-term career benefits of developing a well-rounded background and open-mind.

The Right Attitude.

From a raw materials standpoint, such as IQ, computer skills, and English language ability, young mainland professionals today are demonstrating a very high standard. They've been exposed to globalization and state-of-the-art technologies that are changing the world, much more so than those preceding them even just a few years ago. They are a part of the fastest/quickest/best generation. But it is important that they look beyond themselves and a "me-centered" mentality.

When multinational executives talked about what can make the biggest difference in an employee's success or failure, many singled out one intangible quality in particular. It's having the right attitude. They stressed this as a key success factor, especially for positions requiring frequent interaction with colleagues and clients. They are wary of those who carry an air of superiority, just because of their educational background or English fluency.

"Attitude is always number one with me. I need the combination of Chinese and international skills, but I only want employees who have exceptional attitudes, " states Allan Kwan, former general manager of Motorola's paging system's China operation in Beijing.

Allan shares one experience of his in hiring three mainland returnees from the U.S., who were brought on board as junior managers on his corporate staff. On their first day, he told them that they would be closely judged by their local colleagues. "I let them know that as young returnees in high profile roles, they were going to be especially scrutinized by their peers," he recounts. "Therefore, above all else, their number one priority was to demonstrate their value. They had to outwork their counterparts, and bring to the organization a higher level of thinking and performance. I also told them that it was important for them to make themselves available to others."

"What happened? During our first company outing, the three clustered together and separated themselves from everyone else. This reflected exactly how they conducted themselves in the office as well. There was little effort made to associate with their colleagues on their part. To others, they gave off the impression that they felt that they were better than everyone else. As a result, they never ended up fitting in."

"In a multinational, you have to be aggressive. You have to take initiative, and often function independently. But you can't forget the importance of relationships and working with others, at all levels, in getting things done. It's important to take on your colleagues as equals. If you don't, they'll just say, 'screw you.' Eventually, all three failed because they couldn't gain the support of the other local staff in the company, the ones who they needed help from the most."

No Superiority Complex

When asked about what it takes to be successful in China, James Yao is also very clear. "In my experience, to do well in China you need to take an interest in the well-being and success of those around you," he says. "That's rooted in having a compassion for others."

James spent three years in the mid-90s, as the deputy managing director for Oracle Systems in Beijing. He believes that the time he spent to get to know his staff helped greatly in his ability to elicit their best efforts. "The worst thing you can do is to display a superiority complex to your colleagues. Those who do are bound to fail," he says frankly. "Hey, speaking another language well like English does not make you a better person. You need to demonstrate to others that you care. That will translate into sensitivity, which translates into employee effort and teamwork. That's how you get results."

Perspective and Self-awareness

When managers mention "the right attitude," what they are really talking about is having a good perspective. They want staff who are open-minded, flexible, and credible. These things have a tremendous influence on how quickly a person can learn and how well they will work with others. From a management point of view, it relates to how trainable and accountable a person will be.

Another executive summarized his advice to young professionals in one word: self-awareness. "Many professionals in China lack a self-awareness about themselves.

They don't "get" what they should know or what they should be doing to get a better result for themselves," he says. "For instance, some people place an overemphasis on intelligence and credentials, when it's really effectiveness and results that matter most when doing business. Or some put all their effort into working hard, without taking the time to figure out how they can work smarter."

"Some people place an overemphasis on intelligence and credentials, when it's really effectiveness and results that matter most when doing business."

One Foot In Asia, One Foot In The West

The rapid growth of multinational operations has created a tremendous demand for talent that can respond to the way business is done here. However, identifying enough of the right backgrounds is a major limiting factor for the success of many multinationals in China. Mainly, professionals are needed who can think globally and execute locally. After placing one mainland marketing manager with a consumer electronics multinational in Shanghai, the company's general manager looked at me and simply said: "That's exactly the type we're looking for - people with one foot in Asia and one foot in the West!"

The Ideal Candidate

Today, the ideal candidate for multinational companies in China is more well-rounded, internationally-oriented, and versatile than what they hired just a few years ago. They have quality educational backgrounds, high personal values, bilingual abilities, work experience with reputable companies, and expertise in key functional areas, such as marketing, sales management, and operations. In addition, they have the understanding, open-mindedness and ability to bridge two business cultures and communicate well with management and overseas headquarters. They are also hands-on and resourceful. In particular, highly sought candidates can envision and execute a corporate strategy, develop markets and business opportunities, and launch new products and services in China. It's a combination of talent that international companies are actively trying to identify much more of.

The Ideal Candidate

Education: *Degree from a reputable university. MBA a plus, but not a must.*

Work Experience: *Two or more years of previous work experience with a leading international or reputable company (i.e. Fortune 1000 business). Some experience working both in China and abroad, if possible.*

Professional Skills: *Strong functional specialties (i.e. consulting, operations management, product management, marketing, marketing communications, strategic planning, market research, human resources, finance, accounting, project management, etc.).*

Language Skills: *Excellent spoken fluency in English. Reading and writing a plus.*

Intangibles: *Ability to think creatively and resourcefully. Fast learner. Works well independently. Good communicator. International business perspective. Open-minded. Equally comfortable and effective working in both local and western business situations. Hard worker. Team player. High integrity and personal values.*

Hiring Preferences
The Young And The Trainable

Executives I spoke with directed most of their comments and advice to mainland professionals in their early-20s to mid-30s, referring to them as "the future of China." In their eyes, younger mainland professionals tend to be more achievement-oriented and interested in getting things done. They are more optimistic. From their perspective, the pie is much bigger than how older mainlanders view career opportunities that are available to them.

Meng-hui Chen is the former general manager of Eastern China for Unisys in Shanghai, where she led an organization of over 60 systems integration and application solutions professionals. Recently, she has founded her own applicatiion solutions company called vTradeEx. From her experience, if someone is over 35 years old and has been working in a Chinese enterprise for eight or more years, then she is reluctant to hire them. "They tend to be more political and power oriented," says Meng-hui. "For many of them, they see a pie that is limited, and they are unwilling to give up their share. Their outlook is, if I don't eat you alive, then I'll get eaten alive."

Meng-hui prefers those under 35, who have worked in the international department of an SOE or participated in joint venture projects with international parties. She believes that, at still a relatively early stage in their career and with some international business exposure, they still have the ability to adapt to an international company culture and manner of doing business. She is also open to hiring personnel from Chinese enterprises if she is looking for someone with lots of specific domain or industry knowledge. For instance, several of her sales managers had years of experience with mainland companies before joining her team. "These are professionals in their early 30's who bring with them an extensive network of government and ministry relationships. They understand how to work with these organizations to attain results," Meng-hui points out. "They also know Chinese customers inside and out. If carefully screened, they can be very good. My operation had quite a few senior sales people with these backgrounds who did very well in our organization. However, such hires still imply a lot of training and a change in their mentality."

Well-Rounded Backgrounds

Rather than seek staff from Chinese companies, however, Meng-hui prefers to go "fresh," and recruit and train younger mainland staff. Like most multinational managers and human resources professionals, she looks beyond grades alone. In her experience, students who were more active with outside activities at their university are often better hires. "I don't always look for the best students. They don't necessarily make the best employees, " says Meng-hui. "Instead, I like the ones in the middle one-third of their university. They didn't study the hardest, but they were clearly academically competent. Their most attractive characteristic is that beyond their studies, they enjoyed exploring different things in life, like sports, music, or other student activities. They might not have gotten the best grades, but

"I don't always look for the best students. They don't necessarily make the best employees."

their diverse interests and perspective makes them more resourceful, well-rounded, and creative as employees working in the real world."

Grounded And Independent

Finally, Meng-Hui likes to hire good students from second tier universities. Whereas, many top tier university graduates may be conceptual and theoretical, those who did not attend the most prestigious schools often respond better to challenging, less structured situations. Having gone to a smaller school, advantages have not always been handed directly to them. Instead, they've had to figure out and develop for themselves hands-on skills and a resourceful attitude to get to where they are.

"Many graduates I meet from top universities have an inflated sense of self-worth," she points out. "Unless they possess a strong sense of humility, they end up being powerhouse employees who are too self-promoting and self-focused, and who do not respect the organization. They can be difficult to please and retain. Those from good, but less prestigious universities tend to be more down-to-earth. They can better appreciate the opportunities that are presented to them."

Sheridan favors staff from rougher backgrounds. "Many kids from well-off upbringings have others to ask about everything and to make decisions for them. Many have still not outgrown their parents. As a result, they often look to others to solve their problems," he says. "When they get into unfamiliar situations, however, they feel lost or lack resourcefulness. On the other hand, kids from less privileged upbringings grow up more independently. They've had to deal with a lot of situations on their own at an early age, which helps them in facing new challenges when they get older. That's an important quality for young professionals that I look to train and develop in my organization."

Being successful in the business world requires intelligence for sure. But it also requires good people skills, an ability to read and respond appropriately to situations, and a big picture perspective. These things are not developed and learned from just reading books or attending class. As a result, don't underestimate your own personal background and outside interests. They are important, attractive assets to many international companies. If you can convey your resourcefulness, caliber, and maturity during an interview, many multinational employers will sense that you will make a capable performer in their organization.

A Caution to Chinese MBAs

This past year, I have given many career development presentations at leading mainland MBA programs, including visits to People's University, Beijing University (the BIMBA program), Fudan University, and Jiaotong University (the CEIBS program). The first thing I tell the MBAs I meet is that their future is extremely promising. They should feel very good that they are attending a top mainland business school, at a time when Chinese professionals with international-caliber business training are in high demand. They are in a prime position to develop themselves as future business leaders operating both inside and outside of China.

However, I also have a caution for them, one that can have a severely adverse affect on their road to success. It is a criticism that is surprisingly consistent among the many executives I spoke with who have dealt with MBAs coming out of mainland business school programs. "The biggest weakness of these relatively young MBA programs is that they are too anxious and aggressive about building an elite mindset, one that says their program and their students are the best," describes an executive who has recruited at several top MBA programs in China. "Everyone is trying to shout out loud about how good they are. Rather than having a positive impact, it's creating an incredible arrogance in many of their graduates. Sure, these MBAs are well exposed to functional skills and business scenarios through case studies, but with such an inflated attitude, you have to have serious concerns about their leadership and management potential."

"The biggest weakness of these relatively young MBA programs is that they are too anxious and aggressive about building an elite mindset."

Too Arrogant

Sheridan Yen echoed the same opinion. "In my experience in hiring and managing mainland MBAs, they tend to have the attitude that they are the best," says Sheridan Yen. "In actuality, however, they've had little operating experience. Even the professors who have taught them have had little hands-on experience. As a result, coming out of their programs, they lack depth in their understanding of real business situations. These MBAs love to argue with you, but their limited experience in handling real-life assignments makes you wonder if they can actually execute, or not."

As a result, many fresh MBAs graduates join companies with an aggressive mentality that is not reality-based. Because their pride is so high and because they think that they're already on top, they have a harder time than they should continuing to learn and improve themselves once they start working again. Sooner or later, many place themselves in situations where they fail or can't get things done like they thought they could.

Overestimate Themselves

Lillian Liu is the human resources director for China for one of the U.S.'s largest computer manufactures. She has also had this experience while interviewing MBAs from top mainland business schools. "They learn a lot of academic theory, but when they graduate and look to join a multinational company, they no longer want to get their hands dirty," says Lillian. "They all tell me that they want to do strategic planning or business development. However, when I ask them what does that mean or involve, they can't articulate it."

Or they overestimate their knowledge of what they know. "After joining our company for less than a month, one recent MBA hire came to speak to me about reorganizing our sales department," Lillian continues. "I really had to question how he expected to do this, given that he barely knew our products, our company structure, customer needs, or competitive environment. It was almost funny, but he was entirely serious."

Many mainland MBAs also feel that their business school program has automatically trained them to be good managers. However, even in the United States, most MBAs are hired on as management trainees immediately after graduation. Business schools provide excellent functional skills training and a broader business perspective. Being a good manager, however, is largely about dealing with people. It's about understanding and responding to the needs of your staff. That isn't learned in the classroom, or from textbooks. Rather, being given the opportunity to manage has to be earned. And doing it well takes years to learn for most.

The "Do I Have What Is Needed To Succeed In A Multinational Company" Self-Assessment Quiz

Now that you have a better idea of the type of people that are most suitable for a multinational company, let's make your assessment of yourself for such a position even simpler. The following is a quick self-assessment quiz that will help you determine whether getting into and developing a successful career in a multinational firm is likely for you, or not.

1) *You want to work for a particular multinational company because:*

    a) the company is well-known and offers a good salary

    b) the company offers you a good opportunity in which the position and responsibilities give you the chance to develop your skills and gain greater exposure to an industry that you are interested in.

2) *When it comes to your English language skills, you can:*

    a) carry on a 30-minute conversation fairly comfortably ... as long as the other person sticks to topics about your family, educational background, and hobbies.

    b) handle a typical business situation with a native English speaker without much difficulty.

3) *You like a working environment where:*

    a) you are not required to do much more than what you are told, and where you can manage to survive by looking busy, without actually doing much.

    b) you are encouraged to get involved in and explore different areas, and where your only limitation is how motivated you are to learn and try new things.

4) *During the weekly staff meeting, your boss asks for ideas on how your department can better service your company's customers. You:*

    a) quietly ponder the ideas you have in your head to yourself, and wait to discuss them with your boss after the meeting is over.

b) you share your ideas in the meeting so they may be discussed and receive feedback and opinions from others.

5) *You discover a way to respond faster to your company's customers that will also help save time for other staff in your department. You:*

a) keep what you know to yourself in order that you can outperform your colleagues and be noticed by your management.

b) share this information with your colleagues so that they, and the company, can benefit from your insight.

6) *Whenever you have an idea that you'd like for your boss to know about, you:*

a) stop him wherever and whenever you can and proceed to talk to him about your ideas.

b) you deliver your idea to him in a brief, written proposal that highlights its benefits and costs, providing him with a short summary of key points that he can review on his own time.

7) *You are working on a project and facing a problem that you are having trouble solving. The problem is halting the progress and endangering the successful outcome of the project. You:*

a) try to maintain the appearance that things are going fine, and avoid running into your manager who will certainly want to get a status update on the project.

b) Seek out your manager's help by letting him know of the situation and the difficulties you are having in working out the problem with the project.

8) *You are weighing two job offers. One is for more money, but the person you'll be working for does not appear interested in exposing you to areas that will benefit your career. The other offers less money, but provides a chance to get involved with a new technology that you want to learn more about. You should:*

a) take the higher paying job, because it will offer you the most immediate financial payoff at this stage in your life.

b) take the job that offers you the best means for you to develop your career in a direction that is most interesting to you.

9) *Your company treats you well, and intends to promote you after you've spent a little more time in your current position so you can gain some additional experience supervising staff. At the same time, another company is offering you a title that is two levels above your current one. You:*

 a) jump to the other company because it will be very impressive to have such a big title at your age, even though you could use more time to develop your leadership and management skills.

 b) do an honest self assessment to determine your readiness for taking on significantly greater management responsibilities at this stage in your career, and do what is best for your personal and professional growth and long-term success.

10) *As a manager in your company, your team has under-performed in its ability to reach its quarterly targets. You:*

 a) try to single out the individuals on your team who are not performing to expectations, and report them to your boss.

 b) take responsibility for your team's poor performance, and try to provide greater assistance that will help those who are under-performing to deliver better results.

11) *Your department has been having problems recently resolving a particular customer issue. The problems have long been known among those in your department. In response, you:*

 a) Remind your department manager of the problem by discussing its details whenever you see him.

 b) Try to identify and offer possible solutions that will help solve the problem.

12) *Your boss calls you into his office to tell you that he notices that you are not attaining the results that he feels you should be. Upon hearing this, you:*
   a) Immediately begin to defend your performance, or lack of results, by putting forth outside factors that come to mind that would excuse your recent performance.
   b) Listen to his feedback and try to determine, understand, and assess further what factors he feels might be causing your drop-off in performance.

Self Assessment Ratings

If you selected 10-12 b) responses, then your company's senior management should be closely tracking your career development! Your career goals, personality, and professional maturity appear to be well-suited for success in a multinational company. It should only be a matter of time before you are recognized by your management for opportunities that will offer you the type of career success you seek.

If you selected 7-9 b) responses, don't assume with any certainty your corporate success in a multinational company yet. There are some limitations in how you approach your job and career. Take a good look in the mirror. Put some more time into a deeper, honest self-assessment to determine whether you have the right perspective, attitude, and understanding of what is needed to succeed in a multinational firm.

If you selected 6 or less b) responses, don't give up your contacts with those you know working for a Chinese enterprise. You should prepare yourself for some initial frustration and disappointment in seeking employment in an international company. Until you can expand your understanding of what's going on around you, it is likely that many of the opportunities within a multinational firm, or moving up into the management ranks (should you get into an international company) are going to pass you by. For now, you need to work much harder at developing your professionalism and gaining a broader, deeper perspective of international business practices and concepts.

Chapter 9   Making Good Career Decisions

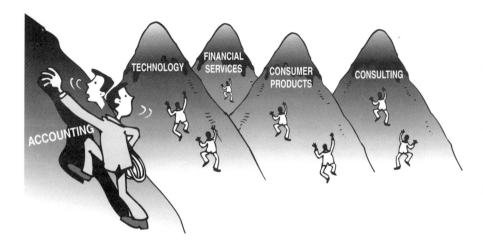

The past several years have been an unprecedented period for mainlanders striving to improve their standing in life through new career options in emerging industries and expanding international companies. With a narrow focus and determination, mainland professionals have set out to diligently reach out and attain opportunities placed before them, as if climbing a steep mountain one step and one handhold at a time.

After several years of hard work, and a concentrated effort that has brought them a degree of success, they now find themselves halfway up the mountain. This has given them time more recently to pause, lift up their head, and look around to see where they are exactly. Suddenly, however, many are coming to a realization that they are having difficulty in moving much higher. Many more are discovering an even harsher reality. Although they have achieved what they initially sought, which was to go higher than where they were before, after all the effort and energy spent, many are discovering that after all these years they may be climbing the wrong mountain. They are realizing that the mountain and objectives that they'd rather be pursuing, which are better suited for them and which might bring them greater satisfaction and success, is actually not the one they're on, but a completely different one. It's an alarming position to find yourself in.

To avoid such a scenario, mainland professionals need to be more proactive in managing their careers at an early stage.

Establish a Career Objective

In June of last year, my partner and I began writing a column called *Ask Wang & Li*, featured in the career section of Netease's Chinese language website (www.163. com). The column provides advice that responds to actual questions received from mainland users regarding their career development and job search issues. After doing the column for several months, it became clear to me that many mainland professionals today lack basic guidance and direction when it comes to making critical career decisions. This is seen in their questions that repeatedly ask us to help determine what is a good industry, job, and company choice for them, and to let them know how to go about making such decisions in the first place.

With the rapid pace of new developments taking place in China's business landscape today, mainland professionals need to be more proactive in managing their career and creating their own opportunities. Many are finding themselves uncertain and confused about their future. "My colleagues and I put most of our focus and energy into performing in our jobs," began one mainland woman in her mid-30s. She is a key accounts manager for a leading international telecommunications company. "Once into an excellent situation like coming to a multinational, we know how to work hard and demonstrate our dedication. After a certain stage, however, it can become frustrating and hard to know what steps to take next to advance our career to the next level. Many of us are in the same boat. Up until now, we haven't put as much thought into what we should be doing for our long-term success. We're not even sure if we're in a good situation or are making the right decisions for ourselves."

"We know how to work hard and demonstrate our dedication. After a certain stage, however, it can become frustrating and hard to know what steps to take next to advance our career to the next level."

Where Do You See Yourself

Whenever we interview candidates for our multinational clients, at some point we want to know where they might see themselves several years down the road. The answer provides insight into how well thought out a person is about their career. Many candidates respond with a vague statement like, "I want to be in management, ... or, I want to work for a leading multinational company." Or, when asked what they seek in their next job, they respond that they are "looking for a good opportunity", without actually being able to define what a "good opportunity" means to them. Unfortunately, such responses shed little light onto a candidate's interests or intentions. Instead, it reflects a lack of thought given to their professional goals.

As an example of what having a good career plan can do, a former classmate of mine discovered early on that he liked the fast-paced world of securities trading. He knew he wouldn't enjoy working in a large, structured corporate environment. Instead, he dreamed of running his own business someday. During summers holidays from his university studies, he worked as an order runner on the exchange floor. Upon graduation, he sorted through offers from top brokerage houses, but chose instead to begin his career as a trading assistant with a small market-making firm. Six years later, he and two former colleagues established their own partnership. Today, he is well on his way to attaining his goal of managing his own company.

Admittedly, few of us have the foresight that my classmate had. The main point is that he was able to determine an objective early, and gradually worked his way towards achieving it. Each career decision he made added an important, additional piece to his background that brought him one step closer to his dream. Too frequently, mainland professionals make career moves on an adhoc basis. They react to what seems like a good opportunity, without putting much consideration into the long-term impact the move will have on their overall career plans. In the many successful careers I've seen, determining career objectives and charting a plan in line with those objectives has helped those people attain the experience and skills that allowed them to reach their goals.

Career Planning

To develop a career plan that responds to your objective, start by envisioning the time frame you'd like your goal to happen in and work backwards from there. Identify the target situations and specific accomplishments that will help move you towards your objective. For example, if you want to manage an office location in China of a major international advertising agency by age 35, what will it take to prepare yourself to achieve such a result? What experience should you gain to help you build the skills and knowledge required to be successful at such a level? Where should you work, with whom, and for how long? What kind of network of contacts and resources do you need to build? Outside of the workplace, what other situations can offer you the training and exposure that will help your development? Determining the answers to these questions are a good beginning to putting together a solid career plan.

Whether you wish to start your own company or manage the mainland operation of a Fortune 500 multinational company, determine your objective early on and come up with steps that will help you meet it. The career path you follow to gain that objective will become clearer along the way. To make a simple comparison, you would never travel to a far-off destination without a map to help direct you. Why begin your career without one?

Do A Self-Assessment

Among the many questions we receive from mainland professionals, the most often asked one relates to how to determine one's suitability for a particular career. Some want to know of a method they can use that evaluates a person's orientation and potential, and that can determine their most suitable career choice.

Although there are personality tests and questionnaires that help people determine what career is most suitable for them, they are primarily designed to help a person know and understand who they are. However, an honest, self-assessment can be done on your own as well. It merely requires that you put some real thought into what you enjoy doing, and into what your personal strengths are. Although these seem to be two of the most basic questions that you should be asking yourself, it is surprising how many people early in their career do not raise them.

Conducting A Self-Assessment For Your Career

- *What do you enjoy doing the most?*
- *What things in life interest you the most?*
- *What are you **ESPECIALLY** good at?*
- *What are currently your greatest skills and assets?*
- *What areas do you feel you need to work on in order to achieve your career goals?*
- *What type of environment or situations will help you acquire those things you need to work on?*

What Do You Enjoy Doing?

A young software engineer wrote in recently to express her concern about her future. She had just started her job and was already feeling the intense competition from the other engineers in her company. She wanted to know if she would be better off finding a new job that was better suited for her, or to keep working hard in her current position. My advice to her hinged on one question and perhaps the greatest factor that determines what a person should do with regard to selecting their career. That is, did she enjoy being a software engineer? Because if the answer was no, then I believe it will be very difficult for her to be an excellent and, ultimately, very successful one.

Personal Travelogue

A Close Call

When I was 26 years old, after I knew that I no longer wanted to continue my career as an engineer and before I moved to Asia, there was a period of time when I decided that I wanted to become a lawyer. I even took the qualifying exam and applied to law schools. My idea back then was to represent the poor and underprivileged, and battle injustice in the courtroom. The image I had of being a lawyer was heroic and full of idealism.

While I was waiting to hear back from law schools, however, I sought out and spoke with several lawyers who were practicing law. With each one, the story was the same. They all enjoyed law school and felt the coursework to be both interesting and challenging. But being a lawyer was a different story. Although it offered them a sound career, none of those I talked to enjoyed their jobs. Like me, they initially had a romantic view of what practicing law was all about. They also envisioned themselves participating in dramatic courtroom cases and working on exciting corporate deals.

Once they began practicing law, however, the reality was much different. Most spent the majority of their time performing research and looking through volumes of documents and books filled with legal cases. They painstakingly reviewed legal contracts, or filled out and submitted applications for clients. When they described their jobs, the work sounded quite repetitive and tedious. None of them talked about their jobs with any type of passion or pleasure. It became apparent to me that the type of drama and excitement that is often glamorized did not exist for the overwhelming numbers of those who actually practiced law.

I'm not trying to imply that a law career is not a rewarding and fascinating pursuit. In my own case, however, I no longer felt that my personality and personal objectives were well suited for it. Because of these conversations, by the time I received my acceptance to law school, I had made the decision not to attend. It would have been the wrong field for me. A year later, I attended business school instead.

To help you know what you might enjoy, talk to people from different industries and in other job functions to understand what they do for a living. One of our best employees joined us just over three years ago. He actually came to our company as a candidate seeking help in finding a job with one of our multinational clients. During his interview with our search consultant, he casually asked her, "do you mind if I ask what it is that you do?" Happy to see this person express an interest in what our company did, our consultant proceeded to describe to him our business and industry, our approach to serving multinational companies and job seekers, and what she enjoyed about her job. Although he had never considered a career in recruitment before, he liked what he heard. He liked the people interaction aspect, diversity in learning about different industries and careers, and exposure to business trends across the entire Greater China region. One week later, we made him an offer. Today, he manages our Hong Kong office.

Those you speak with could be friends, ex-classmates, or just interesting people you meet who seem to enjoy their jobs. Find out about their industry, day-to-day tasks and responsibilities, and why they enjoy their work. Speaking with others about their job is a good way to find out what might appeal to you too.

One executive helps his staff determine what direction and decisions they should take with their career by asking them to think about the two or three times when they were really happy performing in a work situation. Was it when they were involved in closing a deal? Or when they were able to solve a difficult operational problem? Or putting together and producing a report for management? Whatever they were, he believes that they are good indicators that will help tell them what it is that they might be happy pursuing as a career.

Ben Ji: Let Me Entertain You

Personal History: *33 years old. Born and raised in Beijing*
Parents:
Education: *B.A. in International Journalism from the Institute of*
    International Relations

Ben Ji guides his career by one simple concept. That is, no matter what, he pursues opportunities that strike a balance between his personal and career interests. Ben's interests happen to be in the media and entertainment industry.

From the very first stage of his career, Ben has moved a step closer to his entertainment interests with each opportunity presented to him. As a

Ben and wife enjoying rural China

graduate in international journalism, Ben landed a position as an assistant account executive for China Global Public Relations Company, a subsidiary of Xinhua News Agency. The move was his gateway to the media industry. His initial idea in entering this position was to further his education and experience in journalism.

Being a new industry to China at the time, Ben was among the first public relations (PR) professionals in China. Foreign public relations companies had not yet come to China. But Xinhua had a joint venture relationship with Bursten Marsellar, which provided their mainland partner with professional pr training and expertise. Over the next five years, Ben rose to the title of account director. More importantly, through his work he developed an in-depth knowledge of how the Chinese media operates and gained valuable exposure to international business practices. Multinational clients that he serviced included Coca-Cola, Motorola, Daimler-Benz, and Acer Computer, to name a few.

After five years, however, Ben felt himself growing tired of public relations. Although he was successful at it, it was not his true interest. At the time, he received a call from The Walt Disney Company, which was just setting up its operation in the mainland. It was a big break for Ben. He was recruited by Disney in July 1996, as their first mainland staff in China. Disney had expertise in film distribution, which was quite new to China. They needed someone who could apply this expertise to the local market.

Ben was that person. He helped set up the first profit sharing system between foreign film makers and local film distributors. After one and a half years, he joined the Disney's TV business, ABC TV, to diversify his exposure and learn a different arm of the entertainment industry. "My experience at Disney gave me a valuable international perspective, and allowed me to gain ideas that go beyond what is being done in China alone," says Ben. "I've found that to be extremely helpful now that I am developing new business and revenue models for China in my current position."

Today, Ben is the Vice President and General Manager of StarVi.com, an Internet start-up that he joined in March of 1999. StarVi.com focuses on entertainment information and solutions, and represents mainland stars such as Gong Li, Chow Yun Fat, and Zhang Zi Yi. Ultimately, Ben would like to move from the management side to the production side of the entertainment industry. Someday, he would like to start his own business and attract foreign investors and partners. Although he knows he will need to expand his international management skills and market knowledge, he believes he is in an excellent position to realize his dream.

"During the time I was thinking about leaving Xinhua, I got a lot of PR agency offers. Several were highly tempting in their responsibility and compensation. But I knew pr was not what I wanted to do any longer. The entertainment industry is what excited me. Even outside my work, I was always spending my time reading novels and seeing movies. At the time, media and entertainment was a small industry in China. At such an early stage, I knew there would be chances to get involved in many aspects of the industry that someone at my age normally wouldn't be exposed to. Fortunately, that's exactly what has happened."

Beyond doing what interests you, Ben also believes it is most important to develop a depth of knowledge in an industry if you expect to be able to think strategically and have an impact in that field. "That depth is not something that can be accumulated in just three or four years," says Ben. "Once you determine what it is you enjoy, stick with it. You might lose some opportunities in the short-term, but in the long-run you'll see much greater success."

What Do You Feel You Can Be Great At?

The other question we always ask candidates is, what do they feel they are especially good at? We want to know what their special qualities and strengths are, that they believe distinguishes them in an exceptional way from others. These areas are also referred to as your "competitive advantage."

Unfortunately, many mainlanders I have met appear to be a poor match for the career they are pursuing. Some are professionals who demonstrate excellent communication and outgoing people skills, but who have jobs that confine them to a desk all day as accountants or software programmers. Others might be customer service professionals who are shy, or sales professionals who do not like the whole process and pressure of negotiating and closing deals. As one human resources director put it, "there are no such thing as good or bad personalities, or good or bad jobs. But there are good or bad personality fits for certain jobs."

I've even experienced this kind of personality and skills mismatch early on in my own career. Actually, I am a mechanical engineer by training. For the first five years of my career, I worked as a design engineer in a well-known, international toy company. Although it was an excellent position that offered promising opportunities, I knew that a career as an engineer was not utilizing, and would never utilize, my greatest, natural talents. As a result, I knew that I'd never be exceptional at it.

Although I did not know back then what I wanted to do in the future, I did know that I am a people-oriented person. I like dealing with others. And I am good at giving advice and providing insight into situations. As an executive recruiter and career consultant today, I am able to make excellent use of these personal strengths that I possess. As a result, I am now doing each day what I believe I am best suited for.

For many mainland professionals I meet, they are clearly smart and hardworking enough to be good at many things. But as your life and career progress, the question many wish to answer is not so much what can you be good at, but what is it that you believe you can be really great at?

Personal Travelogue

Becoming The Best At What You Do

When I was 26 years old, I worked for Mattel Toys in the U.S., the world's leading toy company. I remember receiving a corporate gift for passing my fifth year anniversary with the company. It was a pewter beer mug that I picked out of the corporate gifts catalog. At the time, I was on a fast-track career climb, having received three promotions in five years. The company was an excellent one. The people were great. The work environment was fun. And the projects I was involved with were always challenging and new.

Yet, I was unhappy. Although I had earned my university degree as a mechanical engineer, I knew I was not interested in being one any longer. My decision to choose mechanical engineering as a career vocation was a highly logical one that I made while in school. I was good at math and science. An engineering degree was a solid profession that would provide for stable job opportunities down the road. It didn't matter that I didn't enjoy or even have an interest in the field, the degree would secure my future. And that's exactly what it did.

After working for five years as a design engineer, however, I knew that I was not an exceptional one. And that bothered me a great deal. Although I was good enough to do well in this field, I could no longer stay in this profession. What was very apparent to me was that there were hundreds, even thousands of others who could be doing what I was doing just as well or even better than myself.

This was for two reasons. The first was that I really had no real interest in engineering, or deep desire to be excellent at it. While my peers had hobbies that matched their passion for designing and engineering things, such as working on cars, building and flying model airplanes, and playing with stereo equipment and sound systems, I was interested in none of those things. Not even remotely. I could follow it. I could do it. But I really wasn't into it. The most telling sign was that I was always watching the clock during work hours. And I was always putting so much more thought into what I was going to do on the weekends, rather than what I was doing during the week. To be honest, some of the longest days I've ever experienced were during my days as an engineer.

The second is that in my job, I knew that I really wasn't making use of who I really was and what I felt I did best. I'm a people person. I enjoy and believe I am good at communicating with others. I know how to read situations, and how to identify the main point. I'm creative and have many original ideas. I believed that my talents would be best used working with people in business situations, rather than spending most of my time in front of a computer. Although I wasn't sure what it was exactly that could take advantage of these abilities of mine, I wished to do something that would better utilize my personality and interests on a day-to-day basis.

At the time, many people questioned why I left such a great job and company. They wondered what it was that I was looking for. I left because I knew I was somebody different than what I was trying to be for the past several years. I chose the profession I did for peripheral reasons. Studying engineering came relatively easy to me and offered a secure career. But I didn't enjoy it, in the way that a person should truly enjoy those things that they love in life. From that point on, I decided to pursue things that, above all else, I enjoyed. If I enjoyed it, I knew there was a much greater chance that I'd be very good at it.

This is how I've made all my career decisions since then. The choices I make come naturally now. I've come to trust my instincts on what it is I like and dislike. As a result, it's much clearer to me what will make me happy. I don't worry about success, opportunities, or money. I focus instead on doing whatever it is I am doing well.

Today, I can say that I am much happier now, than I ever was when I was an engineer, even though my surroundings back then were comfortable and my future more identifiable. It's because I feel that I am able to use every day in my work my greatest talents and abilities. It's because I believe in the purpose and value of what I produce each day. And finally, because I have given myself the chance to become the best at what I do.

In looking back, I am glad that I followed my heart, at a time when I was still able to make changes in my career and pursue another line of work. As you get older, you begin to think of things in terms of what is satisfying and meaningful to you. If you pursue those things, then I don't believe you will likely have regrets. At least, that's how it has worked out for me.

Your Career Lasts A Long Time

After passing the entrance examination of the Medical Institute of Huaxi, one young woman wondered whether to become a dentist or a pediatrician. She was weighing which position would give her the better career development opportunity and higher earnings potential. Having already been admitted to medical school, I told her that I was fairly certain her future was somewhat secure, whether she became either a dentist or pediatrician. Everyone needs a dentist, and I believe good pediatricians will always be sought after by caring parents.

Instead, I told her that the question to ask herself was not about which career offered a better development track or better wages. Both will lead to a comfortable, good life. Rather, the most important thing that she should focus on and determine is which profession does she feel she would enjoy doing for the rest of her life. For instance, if she chose to be a dentist, I believe that by age 35 she would be an established, successful professional in that field. But what then? She would still have 15, 20, or perhaps 25 years to spend in this line of work. What if she didn't really enjoy it. That's a long time to be doing something that you have little interest or attraction towards.

I recommended to the woman that she speak to a few people in these two professions. Beyond salary, consider the lifestyle of each one. Consider the challenge to herself and her actual interest in the field. Believe me, when you get older, it becomes increasingly important to be doing those things that are satisfying and meaningful to you. Performing a job day after day that is not appealing to you can make you feel like a prisoner trapped within your surroundings. It can make for many long, unfulfilling, and frustrating days.

My advice for young professionals is not to worry so much about success and money early on in your career. Those results are likely to come as long as you like your job, and are willing to work hard at it. Instead, give yourself a chance to be excellent at what you do. Follow your heart and put some real thought into what it is you enjoy doing most. Becoming really good and successful at something can be as straightforward as that.

Take An Honest Inventory Of Your Skills

Many candidates claim to have keen aspirations to work in a leading international firm. Yet, when you go one step further and ask them about the suitability of their background and skills for being employed in one, they're unable to articulate many. Instead, their responses are short and simplistic:

Candidate: I'm looking for a position in a multinational company that can offer me excellent career opportunities.

Me: *That's fine. There are plenty of those out there. Mind if I ask you a few questions first?*

Candidate: Sure.

Me: *All right, first of all, how would you rate your English skills?*

Candidate: Not very good right now, but I believe that I could improve if I had the chance to practice everyday.

Me: *Right, ... well, what kind of exposure have you had to international business practices or situations?*

Candidate: Not much really, but I do have a commitment to attaining more. I can tell you that I adjust quickly to new environments.

Me: *Okay, … well, have you any outstanding expertise or professional skills that would make you attractive to an employer?*
Candidate: Not exactly, but I'm a fast learner and I'm willing to work very hard.
Me: *Okay, … well, let's see, … that's good, … ummmm, … so, nice weather we're having, don't you think?*

Although your desire may be high, you need to honestly determine what it is you have to offer such a company. Without fundamental language skills, a basic understanding of international business practices, or functional expertise to offer, there are few compelling reasons why you would be attractive to a multinational employer. For candidates like the one above, I have to tell them that realistically they will have a very difficult time finding a suitable position.

The pool of bilingual mainland professionals is not only growing, they are also offering a broader and deeper range of capabilities. For those without genuinely strong skills, the job market is becoming increasingly competitive. For instance, many mainlanders gain their international exposure mostly in classrooms and understanding of business from books. Their professional experience consists of limited encounters with foreign managers. Based on these things, they believe they possess an advantage for finding a suitable position in a leading multinational firm.

Unfortunately, such peripheral backgrounds no longer carry the same weight that they might have several years ago. International exposure, even for those who have studied abroad, does not automatically attract the same attention as before from employers. The quality of your business skills and language abilities have to be very solid. If they aren't, you need to reassess how good your chances are for being employed by a multinational company, and then find ways to improve in those areas.

The Right Career Moves

Over the past few years of advising professionals in Greater China, I've seen many careers stagnate, as individuals hop from job to job that do not lead to where they expected. You should always keep in mind that the career choices you make today have an impact on your future job marketability and your ability to reach your long-term goals. Therefore, make each decision using deliberate, sound judgment. When contemplating a career move, think about how it will fit into your overall career plans. Ask yourself, does this new opportunity bring me any closer to my career goals?

One candidate who spent several years with a consumer electronics multinational, turned down several offers over the years from competitors who wanted him to join them. Eventually, he accepted an offer to manage the Greater China sales and marketing efforts of a smaller, but niche market-leading firm. The decision was an easy one for him because he felt that the regional exposure and experience of working with a less bureaucratic company would better lead him to his goal of starting his own business someday.

In China, where people are easily influenced by outside factors, we see many professionals enter certain industries for no other reason than they hear you can earn a lot of money in it. For example, there is always a strong interest among MBA mainland graduates I meet to pursue an investment banking career. But when asked why, these MBAs have only a limited understanding of what investment bankers actually do, or what skills they possess that would make them successful in this industry. Many are interested simply because they hear that MBAs abroad actively pursue this profession. This is referred to as "herd mentality", or blindly following the course taken by those around you.

One candidate came to us with a resume showing four jobs with four different companies in five years. He was quite proud that he had received title promotions with each job change, which now placed him as a marketing director. The candidate thought that his career moves indicated how highly sought after and, therefore, how good he was. Unfortunately, our clients did not view it in that way. They questioned his ability to remain with an employer for little more than one year, as well as his "value" given his high salary level and lack of significant accomplishments in any one position. The candidate had reached a point where he had to defend the moves and decisions he made every time he interviewed.

Candidates who rush into a career decision can find themselves wondering later if they made the right choice. Making any good career choice takes time and careful consideration, and should weigh not only the present, but also how things might look like in the future.

Choose A Job For The Right Reasons

Recently, a university graduate wrote to tell us that he found it very confusing facing so many job postings when surfing the Internet. How was it possible to select a position? He pointed out that one had to be choosy even in buying clothes, let alone in finding a job. With no influence over a company's popularity, social influence, specific work content, salary and treatment, he wondered how to avoid the blindness when selecting a job? In other words, how should he go about choosing a position and company most suitable for him?

It is particularly important to get into a good development situation early in your career. However, in China, the quality of work environments and what they offer varies greatly. This means finding a company and position where you will be given opportunities to learn and grow, and where you will be under the guidance of strong professionals is crucial. The most important factors to weigh when considering a new position are the people you'll be working under and learning from? What is the scope of responsibilities that the job offers? What other internal and external business areas does the position expose you to? What is the likelihood you will be successful at performing the job? What skills will you learn from the position? Will the experience you gain help lay a strong foundation for your long-term career development?

You should also look at the company's commitment to growing its business in China. Is the operation an established or a start-up one? What is the company's position within its industry? What type of management structure and resources are in place to support you?

Finally, look at the industry and its future potential. Is the industry experiencing growth or at a mature stage? What is the competitive situation in the market(s) you're being asked to develop? If these areas look promising, then the advancement opportunities and financial rewards will present themselves, as long as you are able to prove yourself as a strong performer. This is seen time and time again for countless mainland professionals working for multinationals in China.

Evaluate Job Opportunities On . . .

Position:	*Will you gain skills, exposure, and experience that will add to your future marketability?*
Management:	*Who will be supervising you? Who will you be learning from?*
Company:	*What is the company's commitment and competitive positioning in the region?*
Industry:	*What is the state of the industry you are entering?*
Self:	*What is your overall confidence level that you can do the job well/successfully?*

Too Much Influence From Outside Factors

In Chinese culture, people are always comparing themselves to others. It takes maturity to get past the influence of what others are doing and saying when you are making career decisions. Unfortunately, too many mainland professionals make choices based on reasons that are not substantial. They are attracted to position titles and well-known company names. They emphasize the status of the firm, over the quality of the position and the development opportunities it provides. This is a mistake.

Unfortunately, too many mainland professionals are attracted to position titles and well-known company names. They emphasize the status of the firm, over the quality of the position and the development opportunities it provides.

Finding an excellent opportunity that suits you can present itself in many different scenarios. For instance, I meet many candidates from smaller companies, whose caliber is even above those from larger, more established firms. It's because they have received greater exposure and training through a closer working relationship with their boss, who possesses a well-trained business background.

"When I ask my staff why they like to work for us, most say that it gives them a chance to work for an international company and to learn more things or improve themselves," says the managing director of an events management multinational in Beijing. "Or because it is a place where they can practice and improve their English. Rarely do they say that it's because of their interest in our business or the type of work they do. I tell them that our company can certainly offer many of the opportunities they seek. But to be really successful, I hope that they are able to love what they are doing."

Doing Things That Make You Happy

Joan Lin's striking characteristic is that she is a calm and relaxed person. I would describe her as someone who is at peace with herself. It is quite apparent that she is happy with what she is doing with her life.

Joan is the manager of a company that manufactures safety reflective adhesives, that are used in hospitals and road signs, for the entire country. She has been with her company, for the past eight years. In fact, she began her career with the company.

During that time, she has created and then assumed each position she has been promoted to. "When I began, the company wasn't even sure if there was a market in China for the product they wanted me to work on," recalls Joan. "They were so uncertain that they only hired me on a temporary, six-month contract. It was up to me to research and assess the product's market potential, as well as come up with an initial business plan."

Fortunately, her findings and report at the end of the six months convinced management that there was tremendous market potential in China for safety products. But it would take time to educate and develop customers. To perform such a business development role, the company then hired her as an account executive. Over the next eight years, she progressively took on roles that focused on key account sales, sales and marketing supervision, internal and external marketing training, and leadership and management.

To help Joan and her product line reach the next level, she was sent overseas to other markets so she could see the future for China for the product line and come up with the next stages of her strategic plan. At this time, her business focus has evolved into developing the company's local manufacturing capabilities for products she supervises.

With her well-rounded business training and proven success in managing product lines, there are many options in the market available to Joan. Her reasons for continuing along her current path, however, go beyond just the opportunities and responsibilities the company can give her. Her ultimate goal is to do something very meaningful for China. That vision is taking place in her current work and products she is involved in.

"Asbestos dust in the lungs is worse in China than anywhere else in the world," explains Joan. "There are 500,000 mainlanders, mostly factory workers, who suffer from this. This is more cases than the rest of the world combined. Most workers are not even aware of the problem. The key is educating the end-users. I believe I can help do that."

Recently, through Joan's lobbying efforts, her company received the government's directive that gives them permission to draft the standards for the industry on asbestos dust levels in the workplace. She is one step closer to significantly reducing this serious health problem in the country, and seeing the results of her heartfelt efforts and objectives. It's a purpose and understanding of oneself, like in Joan's case, that leads to the type of success that can be most satisfying to you.

Wrong Reason, Wrong Decision

Last year, I met a woman who was the director of operations for a new Internet company. She had graduated from one of China's leading MBA programs in Beijing six months before. She had contacted me to seek help in finding a chief operating officer (COO) for the start-up. After talking about the company's situation for an hour, it was clear that their business had major problems that they were unlikely to be able to solve. Mainly, the company lacked any type of management leadership and business planning. The founder was very strong in the development of technology and could talk enthusiastically about the vision he had for his company. However, even he was without previous management or business experience.

When I asked her why she joined this company, she explained that she had met the founder, who was a professor at her university. When he pitched the potential of his company to her, he told her he was very interested in bringing a bright MBA into his company, and that there were plenty of opportunities for her to help build the business. Having just armed herself with management theories on how to run a business, she was eager to apply what she had learned. "When I was interviewing with companies, I was looking for the highest title I could find. Since the higher the title, the greater the responsibilities and exposure," she reasoned. The opportunity seemed to respond to what she felt she had to offer and what she wanted to do.

When I looked at her situation though, I felt that she was in a very unhealthy position. Within her company, she was the only one with any significant business training. The rest of the 30 or so staff were even more junior than herself. She was able to recognize a lot of the company's problems, but with little actual experience in dealing with such issues, she didn't have the background or support to do anything about them. As a result, there were few means for her to implement or even verify her ideas for improving the business.

I felt that her decision to seek out and join this type of opportunity was a mistake on her part. Her judgment was poor regarding what she was ready to achieve, and what type of experience and environment she needed at that point in her career. The title, responsibilities, and exposure her company offered were adding little to her professional development. There was no guidance, no functional or industry expertise, and no professional practices that existed within the company. She was isolated and lacked access to resources that could help her grow.

Coming out of her MBA program, what she needed was a situation where she could work for someone whom she could learn from. She would have been much better off with an assistant manager's title, under a strong manager and within a company that offered more resources and exposure to leading business practices. At a relatively young stage in her career still, she was clearly someone who needed to gain more practical work experience than someone who was ready to manage a business operation in a complex market.

Early in your career, you don't want to be learning all your lessons by trial and error. And you don't want to find yourself in a situation where you know more than anyone else around you. That's a sure sign that you're in a questionable situation. You'll learn more and faster by being around others more experienced than you who can share with you their knowledge and insights. And that will lead to better scenarios for your long-term success.

Do Your Own Quality Control

With so many job postings out there these days, it is up to you to do your own quality control with regard to what is a good opportunity for you, and what is not. Pursuing a new position is a two-way street. You have just as much at stake as the company you are considering. Your number one objective in any interview is to sell yourself and to get the company interested in you. However, once you've done that you should be thorough in asking your own questions to determine what kind of skills, exposure, and experience you will gain from the position, and how this will happen. At the appropriate time during the interview process, learn as much about the job and the company as you can. This is not being too forward on your part. Such inquiries are the only way to help ensure that you pick a position and company well-suited for yourself. If a prospective employer is resistant or unable to answer such questions, then it's a good indication that they might not be the best employer to work for. Instead, work for someone whom you feel confident is able to support and respond to your career interests and needs.

Know When To Say No

Some job seekers feel pressure to accept the first offer that comes along, even if the position is not in line with their career goals. Turning an offer down becomes even more difficult when the salary package is alluring. Although it never hurts to be flexible, it is important to build on your career plan as much as possible, even if that means turning down a seemingly attractive opportunity. The more in touch you are with your objectives, the better decision you will make when facing an offer for a position you are not sure you should take.

A woman who recently changed jobs called to tell us that she is unhappier now than she was before. As a chemical engineer for many years, she had not felt satisfied with her profession for quite some time. Yet, she accepted an almost identical position with another company simply because she was offered a higher salary. Shortly afterwards, she realized that what she really wanted was a new career, a realization that came a little late. The pressure she faced starting a new job she wasn't excited about could have been avoided had she not made her decision so hastily.

A good example of knowing when to say no happened to a man who came close to accepting a position as head of a company's IT department. Although he had several years of experience as an IT manager, he realized during the interview that he was not qualified for the job. Yet, to his surprise, he was offered the position. Turning the job down was not an easy decision to make. But after learning about the company's more fundamental problems later on, he was glad he did not accept the offer. Apparently, senior management was more concerned with filling the vacancy than they were with understanding their staffing needs. He found out that three other managers had accepted and left the position over the previous twelve months. Because of this, the IT department had been paralyzed for some time. Had he accepted the offer, he would have likely found himself in a situation where he would have had little chance of succeeding.

The point in these examples is to have personal and professional objectives that are as clear to you as possible, and then stay on track in pursuing them. Having even a general plan or some guiding criteria to follow can only work in your favor, as you make career choices that affect your long-term success and happiness.

Job Now, Money Later

Ying Han is very clear on how to evaluate a new position. "When considering a new job, you should always seek know-how first," she begins. "Find a position that allows you to build your competencies and experience. Next, you can consider the image of a company or position. The final consideration should be salary.

Unfortunately, too many young mainland professionals today are prioritizing jobs in just the opposite order."

When considering a job, try not to place the money aspect above all other considerations. We introduced one candidate for a sales manager position in a leading multinational packaged goods company. The candidate had a *When considering a job, try not to place* successful background as a marketing *the money aspect above all other* professional. Although she had no previous sales experience, the client *considerations.* liked her energy and intelligence. The position offered the candidate a chance to learn a new job function, prove herself in a revenue-generating role, and add a valuable element to her career development. It was just the type of position and opportunity she was looking for.

Before the interview, I gave the candidate the compensation range for the position. I let her know that I thought it was a fair amount for her level of experience. In addition, I emphasized that the position offered her an exceptional chance to acquire business development, profit and loss, and management experience. The candidate acknowledged the compensation expectations and her own priority to find a position that offered a promising and attractive career track.

The interview went well and it became obvious that the client was very interested. At the end of the meeting, however, the candidate couldn't resist resorting back to her original view of her value. Thinking that she was gaining the upper hand, she told the client she was only interested in the position if it offered a higher salary. In her mind, she felt that the company should pay her a premium if she was going to give up her current situation for something that would result in a major change in her career.

It was a "what can you do for me" attitude that reflected both a lack of commitment towards her move and an unrealistic assessment of her value and the opportunity. The client was willing to give the candidate the opportunity, if the candidate was willing to share the risk. But he was not interested in paying a premium for someone who was entirely untested in her ability to run a key part of his business. Not surprisingly, the client's interest in the candidate ended right there.

Steven Song: Job Over Money

Personal History: *30 years old. Born in Shanghai and raised in Beijing*
Parents: *Mother and father both from Shanghai*
Education: *B.A. from the Beijing Institute of Chemical Technology*

When weighing his future career options last year, Steven Song was looking at several job offers that would allow him to increase his annual earnings from between 20-40% over his previous position. However, Steven chose his current company, which offered just about the same compensation he was making before.

"If it's a choice between my career development and money, I'll sacrifice the money in the short term every time,

Steven hanging out at his bar, Schiller's, in Beijing

" says Steven with emphasis. "I've always followed that philosophy. I know I can find jobs that pay better, but I chose my current company because of what I felt I could learn in the position. You can always make money doing the things you normally do. But to reach much greater career and financial prospects over the long-term, you need to continually build skills that will take you to the very top."

From the very beginning, Steven's approach to career development has always emphasized what a position could add to his skills, knowledge, and long-term career goals. His first job out of university was as an office assistant in an international telecommunications company. "My title could just have easily been "the guy who does everything that nobody else wants to do,'" jokes Steven. Steven ran around and supported the professional staff in any way he could, including doing a lot of translation work. Interestingly, through his many hours spent translating product and marketing materials, he began learning the company's products.

After six months, he was transferred to the sales department as a sales assistant. Again, the position was a very junior role, in which he did a lot of meeting coordination and sales support. Gradually, however, he began getting chances to meet customers. Most important, the position allowed him to understand and learn the point of view of customers, rather than just how the company tried to sell its products. This gave him the basis for developing his own selling approach.

Steven looks back at his first job as a crucial one in setting his career in the right direction. It allowed him to build strong, core business skills. It also gave him chances to get involved, mature professionally, and gain exposure to high caliber managers whom he could learn from.

In his next position, Steven joined a small international company. "In a smaller operation, you get to see just about everything that goes into running a company," he says. "Management needs to make full use of every employee. That's just the type of environment I was looking for. I could speak directly with the managers whenever it was appropriate. Just by working next to and observing them, you learn so many short-cuts and insights on how to get things done, rather than taking much longer to figure them out by yourself."

"I don't know if I'm necessarily any more or any less ambitious than the next person. But for me, I look at reaching the pinnacle of any objective as just a moment," summarizes Steven. "The road getting to the top is where we all end up spending most of our lives. What I like is waking up each morning knowing I'll be facing new challenges and learning new things. I suppose I'll always have that approach to my life."

The Decisions You Make Now Affect You Later

I've met many mid-career professionals who feel trapped in their job. After eight or ten years in their current industry and professional role, they wish to do something else that would be much more interesting and meaningful to them. They feel uncertain about their future, lack contentment with their jobs, and appear dissatisfied with their lives. Unfortunately, with significant financial and family responsibilities to weigh now, they have reached a stage where a change is unlikely. And the longer they wait, the more difficult a transition becomes.

A decision to enter an industry or take a particular job can have a profound affect on your entire future, as well as your personal well-being. Making good choices regarding your career affects whether or not you will enjoy your work and be successful at your job. It can affect how your life may turn out overall. Therefore, be sure to make your career decisions based on the right reasons, ones that are personal and important to you. It can save you a tremendous amount of time and energy spent trying to get on a career track that is more suitable or desirable for you later on down the road.

Chapter 10　Interviewing Well

Although job search and hiring activity in China is high these days, many mainlanders have had relatively little experience interviewing for new positions. They may have been assigned a position in a state-owned enterprise after graduating from university, or were introduced to their job through personal connections. As a result, job interview skills among many mainland professionals tend to be weak. However, when interviewing with managers from leading multinational companies, being able to talk about and sell yourself effectively, as well as qualify and evaluate new opportunities, are a must.

Presentation and First Impression

When entering a job interview, you want to begin without projecting unnecessary actions or visual cues that may raise questions in your interviewer's mind that work against you. You don't need to sell yourself within the initial impression. That's what the interview itself is for. Rather, the objective of your first impression is not to make a bad one. When first meeting an employer, we stress attention to some basic areas.

Be natural when shaking hands. People interpret a lot from a handshake, reading it as an extension of a person's personality. Always use a firm, confident handshake. You'd be surprised how a weak or clammy one can turn people off. I've met some people who also like to grasp your hand with both of theirs. Although this may show particular warmth in social situations, it is inappropriate in a professional situation. It can come across as overly sincere and presumptuous.

Clients, always tell me that they don't care how a person dresses, as long as it's clean and neat. This refers not only to your clothes, but also hair, fingernails, and even shoes. There is no need to be flamboyant either. One candidate I interviewed wore a tie and shirt so colorful and clashing, it took an effort just to look at him. When I glanced at his feet, his socks were just as eye-catching. It was unnecessary and distracting. People's fashion tastes differ, but your clothing should above all reflect professionalism. That's enough.

Whether consciously or subconsciously, people tend to draw conclusions from simple actions and observations of those they meet for the first time. As such, the non-verbal aspects of your presentation can make a difference in how you may be perceived by an interviewer. With your appearance, the objective is to look professional and competent. You want to give the interviewer the idea that you are someone who is well prepared, sharp, and ready to go. Looking sloppy and unkept does not reflect those things, and can raise concerns about your work habits and professional outlook.

The non-verbal aspects of your presentation can make a difference in how you may be perceived by an interviewer. With your appearance, the objective is to look professional and competent.

For the most part, proper etiquette and good personal presentation are anticipated in any initial encounter. Making a positive first impression is a matter of exhibiting basic courtesy and common sense. Although a poor first impression may not hurt your chances for a successful interview, why create signals that may only harm a person's assessment of you? By simply avoiding things that may disrupt a first meeting, you can consider your first impression to be a good one.

Taboos

Avoid Disruptions

Regarding taboos, one immediately comes to mind. That is, make sure to turn off your mobile phone or pager during the interview. There is nothing more distracting and impolite when interviewing a candidate than a phone interruption. Should you happen to forget and receive a call while being interviewed, then politely apologize to the interviewer, tell the caller that you cannot talk at the moment, and hang up.

During one interview, a candidate received a call and proceeded to speak for five minutes while I waited. I believe he thought I was impressed to see that his customers were so anxious to reach him. Unfortunately, I could only think about how unprofessional he was being. When he finished the call, I immediately finished the meeting. After such a lack of consideration, there was no way I was going to recommend him to any client.

Try Not To Be Too Late/Too Early

Tardiness can also reflect poorly on professionalism, and lead an interviewer to question the overall quality of your business training. With traffic so unpredictable in major mainland cities, however, it's not unusual to show up late for appointments. Of course, if you know you'll be late, telephone ahead if you can and let your interviewer know in advance.

It is not such a big deal to arrive late for an interview. Unless, that is, you don't acknowledge it. If meeting an employer for the first time, you need to make the situation clear. You know you were late. The interviewer knows you were late. To move past it, you just need to acknowledge your tardiness with a brief apology. Detailed explanations are not necessary. But if you don't at least bring it up, then the interviewer does not know whether or not you understand the importance of or care about promptness and, more importantly, your professionalism. By showing some common courtesy in acknowledging any inconvenience to the interviewer, the tardiness is usually quickly forgotten.

At the other end of the spectrum, some candidates unexplainably arrive up to half-an-hour before a scheduled interview. Busy managers hold themselves closely to tight schedules. Arriving too early can reflect a lack of consideration for other people's time, or give a potential employer the impression that you have too much time on your hands or are overly eager. If you are early, wait outside somewhere and use the time for a final mental preparation of what you want to say during the interview. Or, find a mirror for a visual "once-over." Your worst option is to sit awkwardly inside the office, waiting for a long time with little to do.

A no-show without an immediate and credible explanation is a definite no-no. Managers may go to great lengths in arranging their schedule to set up an appointment. We've seen cases where canceled appointments never led to a second chance to meet. One client accommodated a prospective candidate by scheduling a Sunday morning interview. On the morning of the interview, the candidate called to cancel. The client was extremely put out by this failure to keep the meeting, and interpreted a lack of commitment on the candidate's part. In the end, he felt that if making the interview was not important enough to the candidate, then the job must not be that important to him either.

The Salary Question!

Perhaps the biggest taboo that we see mainlanders make is asking about salary during the first interview. Hearing the question in an initial encounter can raise an employer's concerns about a person's priorities and genuine interest in a position. It sends a warning that the person being interviewed places too much emphasis on money and not enough on the job or company itself.

As a candidate, always focus your attention in the initial interview on selling yourself and making a great impression. Let the employer be the one to raise the topic of compensation. There's no point in bringing up the salary question if you haven't successfully convinced them that you're worth hiring in the first place. Be patient. The discussion will come up at the appropriate time, if and when the employer feels it is necessary to talk about.

First Impression Checklist

✔ Make sure you dress in a manner that is clean and neat
✔ Check for anything that can be visually distracting (i.e. dirty fingernails, dandruff on clothes, uncombed or unwashed hair, soiled shoes, etc.)
✔ Shake hands firmly and confidently
✔ Turn off your mobile phone or pager
✔ Apologize immediately and briefly if you arrive late for the interview
✔ Don't arrive to the interview too early
✔ Avoid canceling a scheduled interview if at all possible
✔ Always wait for the interviewer to raise the topic on compensation first

Don't Undersell Yourself

Frequently, I'll interview candidates who have worked for several years and ask them to describe their professional experience and strengths. As they proceed to talk about themselves, they'll say things such as, "I'm very entrepreneurial, … I work well with others, or … I'm very hard working." Hmmm, I'll think to myself. After working for several years, there should be more to say about themselves than that.

For recent college graduates, responses of this nature are not uncommon. After all, young graduates have little to elaborate on by way of actual work experience. At such an early stage in their career, they must emphasize and rely mainly on their outstanding personal qualities and potential in order to impress an interviewer.

For experienced professionals, however, your greatest, most tangible attributes are the professional achievements and experience you have accumulated. In other words, you've done things that can be highlighted. Therefore, use specific examples to emphasize your outstanding qualities to a potential employer. It's the best way to sell yourself in a job interview.

For example, if you want to demonstrate your entrepreneurial quality, draw attention to instances where you have taken initiative, or created something from nothing. Even though you may not have run your own company, perhaps you've initiated projects within your job. Or, you've identified an opportunity and pursued it with nothing more than your ingenuity and resourcefulness. Describe the idea, and how you proceeded. Talk about how you overcame project threatening obstacles. That paints a vivid picture of a true entrepreneur.

Or, if you're hardworking, illustrate situations where you've achieved results while handling several assignments at once. Or instances where your boss specifically selected you for a project that required you to perform on top of your normal responsibilities. If you feel you have good sales skills, elaborate on your performance in this area. Quantify your results relative to your peers. If you've never sold before, identify instances where you've convinced management to buy into an idea or project, or where you've supported the sales efforts of others. By conveying a strong understanding of the sales process, you can impress upon an interviewer that you could be very good in such a role.

Sharing specific examples that provide a sense of what you can achieve is always more impressive and impactful than just using words or phrases that do not reveal any details about your capabilities. In any interview, it's up to you to highlight your excellence in an interesting and vivid way. Once I point out and inquire about areas of their background, I'm usually impressed by many of the things candidates have done when described in greater detail. Don't expect employers to have the same patience in pulling such information out of you though. In most cases, they won't. In a job interview, that's your responsibility.

> *Sharing specific examples that provide a sense of what you can achieve is always more impressive and impactful than just using words or phrases that do not reveal any details about your capabilities.*

Bring Up Your Energy Level

In addition to being somewhat passive when it comes to speaking about themselves, many mainlanders are not aware of their energy level when interviewing, which is often low. I've interviewed many mainland professionals who speak about themselves in a low, monotone voice. Their body language is motionless or slouchy, making them appear small and timid. After a short time, it becomes difficult to take an interest in talking with them further.

Potential employers can understand that you may be nervous during the interview. However, they also want to get a sense of whether you have the maturity, poise, and confidence to handle such a difficult situation. These qualities come across through an energy level and body language that shows you are proactive, attentive, and determined. It is natural to want to speak to people who are interesting and captivating. Displaying some energy and enthusiasm elevates the discussion between you and the interviewer, as well as their level of interest in getting to know you better.

Avoid The Oversell

On the other end of the spectrum, I've interviewed many mainland candidates who oversell themselves by overstating their responsibilities and achievements. Instead of standing behind what they have done as an individual, they glamorize that they are part of a multinational company. Or they draw attention to how much their current company values them, or how highly sought they are by other companies. However, when asked to elaborate further, they are unable to provide credible or specific instances of exactly what it is they've accomplished to be in such demand.

While screening a candidate for a marketing manager position, a candidate bragged to one of our consultants about how successful he had been in his previous marketing positions. In talking about his marketing background, however, he was quite vague about any details. When the consultant asked him if he could describe some of the product launches he had been involved in and the role he played, the candidate responded by saying, "well, there are too many to mention." After a brief pause, the consultant said, "that's okay, describe just one." With little to elaborate on, the candidate exposed his lack of expertise by stuttering through some sketchy recollections of past marketing efforts.

Don't Just Talk, Listen Too!

In another common scenario, we arranged an interview between a mainland candidate and one of our multinational clients. The position and company were both attractive to the candidate. His background displayed the "right" education and experience for the position. On the day of the interview, he walked in with a prepared presentation on why he was perfect for the job. He shared his thoughts on their current strategy and his plans for the company's future business development. Sixty minutes later, the interviewer thanked him for his time and showed him the door. The client did not pursue the candidate further. It was clear that his pitch fell on deaf ears. Where did he go wrong?

Candidates like this one, who get caught up in their enthusiasm towards a job or company, will spend the entire interview "selling" themselves, without ever understanding what the prospective employer is "buying." In this instance, the candidate prepared thoroughly by researching the company and its strategy. He incorporated his own experiences into his presentation. What he did not consider beforehand, or pick up on during the interview, was how such an aggressive "pitch" would be received by the employer.

When we spoke to the client afterwards, he told us that the candidate initially came across as professional and well-prepared. As the interview progressed, however, his single-minded pitch came across as a bit arrogant and presumptuous. He didn't seem to listen or respond to what it was that the interviewer wanted to know. Rather than an interactive dialogue, the candidate gave a one-sided presentation. In his eagerness to make a good impression, he instead made a poor one.

The candidate was too intent upon selling himself, when his resume had already "sold" his interviewer on him. His years of experience with top-tier multinationals and history of promotions already said a lot. From our client's perspective, the candidate wouldn't let go of the selling angle and relate to him at a person-to-person level. To every question asked of him, he responded with yet another account of his successes in earlier jobs. After the third or fourth time this happened, the interviewer found his attention wandering and his patience short. Eventually, he just ended the interview, frustrated at not being able to have a simple, straightforward conservation to get to know the candidate better. Though convinced of his professional capabilities and qualifications, the interviewer never got the feeling that the candidate was someone he could work comfortably alongside of.

Although you may have every reason to be proud of past achievements and want to recount them all to an interviewer, you should maintain an awareness of what the client is interested in knowing about you. Foreign managers often want to gain a sense of who you are as a person. They are not so interested in a well-rehearsed presentation. In an interview, there is a fine line and a distinct difference between "selling yourself" and "over-selling yourself." Successful

Foreign managers often want to gain a sense of who you are as a person. They are not so interested in a well-rehearsed presentation.

job seeking candidates don't cross that line, appropriately seeing it as the difference between further interviews and lost opportunities.

Overemphasis on Academic Qualifications

A human resources manager of a manufacturing plant in Dongguan wanted to know how we checked the validation of a university degree for prospective new hires. Actually, I have to confess that in over seven years of recruiting candidates for multinational employers, I have never been asked to validate someone's educational background. The reason is that a university degree is not the reason why I would recommend to a client to hire a particular person.

Educational background, of course, is an area of a resume that attracts initial attention and often leads to our desire to speak with a candidate. But that's all. For my recruitment company and our clients, a university certificate is merely a qualification that shows that a person is likely to be smart and have solid academic training. Beyond that, however, we rely on the interview process and a candidate's response to practical questions to determine how good they are. These questions relate to their experience, knowledge of business practices, and how they might analyze and handle situations. Regardless of educational background, if the candidate is not impressive in communicating their knowledge and capabilities, then they will not be recommended by us or be hired by the multinational companies we work with.

Many professionals from top universities in China place too much weight on their educational background. No doubt, it gives them an advantage in gaining the interest of employers. When it comes to the actual hiring decision, however, a person's educational background becomes one of the last criteria that is considered.

Go With Your Strengths

Some candidates attempt to get a new job while also seeking out a function or industry that is different from what they've done in the past. These may be sales people who want to do marketing, technology professionals who want to be in front-end, business development roles, or industry professionals who want to be consultants. If you are changing companies, it's a lot to also expect to jump into a different functional role or industry at the same time.

We tell candidates to focus their job search on opportunities that best leverage their existing strengths and experience. Your first and foremost objective is to get yourself into a more beneficial situation for your career. If in changing companies you end up with a less-than-ideal job, it's okay. Once you start working, you can become familiar with the corporate culture and business practices of your new employer. As importantly, you can begin to demonstrate your capabilities, establish a track record of success, and develop the internal support you need to help get you closer to the ideal position you're looking for. It then becomes much easier to switch into another job function or industry. With enough persistence and some patience, it will happen.

Good Questions To Ask?

In a job interview, interviewers will often end the meeting by asking if you have any questions for them. It's a common situation that could have several purposes. The interviewer might want to know what is going through your mind at that moment. He might want to get an idea of how you think, based on the type of questions you ask. He might be looking for a chance to further sell you on the position and their company. Or he may just be being polite, as a way to end the interview.

For you, the offer to ask questions allows you to gain more information to both understand the opportunity and to further sell yourself. If you have good, specific questions about the position, company, or industry you are interviewing for, then you should ask them. However, if you are unsure if your questions are good, then you might want to ask some safer, but still helpful ones.

For instance, many hiring managers tend to think that the best person for a position is someone similar to them. They like candidates who remind them of themselves at an earlier stage in their career. Therefore, a good question to ask is one relating to the interviewer's own background, and in particular, their career development or rise within the company. We worked with one candidate who was having a fairly uneventful interview. The discussion lacked energy and appeared as if it would end early. Towards the end, however, the candidate asked the interviewer about his background and discovered that, like himself, he graduated with an engineering degree. The subject seemed to grab the interviewer's attention, who was fond of this earlier time in his career. The two shared stories of their engineering interests and how their technical training supported their evolving professional goals. By making this discovery, the candidate was able to extend the interview, connect with the interviewer, and give himself another chance to relate his own background to the position.

It is also helpful to ask questions about employees in the position similar to the one you are being considered for. Upon inquiring about the background of others in the sales department she might join, one candidate was able to surmise that the team lacked someone with strong connections in the travel industry that was a key target market for their business. Although she already knew this was one reason why the company was interested in her, it reinforced to her the significance of her experience in dealing with this customer base. In later interviews with other managers, she began placing a heavier emphasis on her travel industry contacts, which helped secure the necessity of her experience to the department. Ultimately, these interviews led to their hiring the candidate.

In any new encounter, the more you can connect with or relate to the other party, the greater your chances are for achieving your objective. The same is true in a job interview. Asking questions is a natural part of the interview process with multinational companies. Particularly with western-trained managers, don't be afraid to ask questions about the people you're speaking with. By knowing their professional background, you can understand better the requirements for the position and can measure the relevance of your own experience against theirs. From this, you can identify key information that can help you emphasize to the interviewer your suitability for the job.

A Major Interview Mistake

A job interview is a two-way evaluation process, with both the interviewer and interviewee probing the abilities, personality, and potential of the other side. Safe to say, however, it's usually the interviewer who has the upperhand. As a result, be sure you successfully sell yourself first before getting too carried away with interrogating the person you're interviewing with.

Although you would think that most people go into an interview with the goal of selling themselves into a position, some people show up with an "impress me" attitude. This can be a dangerous mistake. For instance, sometimes when we introduce a position to a candidate, they'll immediately bombard us with questions regarding compensation and promotion track. They get overly concerned about how they'll be treated by the company.

Reactions like this always surprise me. Instead of being happy about the company's interest in meeting them and inquiring about information on their business that could be helpful in the interview, they want to know about bonuses and raises. "Hey," I remind them, "the company has only expressed an interest in you, not extended you an offer. We don't even know if they'll like you yet."

We've seen instances where too many probing questions, too early in the interview process, turned off the employer. In one case, we introduced a candidate for a management position he was well qualified for. From the beginning, however, rather than focusing on the opportunity, the candidate's main concerns were about what the company could do for him. He went into the initial interview armed with questions about salary and the promotion track. At the same time, he showed only lukewarm interest in sharing information about himself, not wanting to reveal too much until he was sure the company could offer him what he wanted.

As the interview progressed, he began to realize that the company culture, product line, and management were all attractive to him. He contacted us afterwards to say that he was excited about the position and was very interested in the job. But when I followed up, the interviewing manager was not interested in the candidate. He felt the candidate was too interested in quick promotions, and did not appear interested enough in the position itself. He added that by the end of the interview, he still didn't have a good idea about what the candidate could do. It was too bad, because it was well within the candidate's capabilities and work experience to sell himself for the position.

Evaluating a company and its benefits to you is a necessary step when looking at a new position. However, don't get too far ahead of yourself by being too coy early on in the interview process. Your first and foremost objective is to impress your interviewer(s) and to get them to want you for the position. Once you've succeeded in doing that, then any topics that are on your mind are up for discussion. It becomes much easier to raise issues like compensation, once the prospective employer's objective has shifted from trying to evaluate you, to trying to attract you. By focusing on and talking about more sensitive topics too soon, you may end up without any options to weigh.

Your first and foremost objective is to impress your interviewer(s) and to get them to want you for the position. Once you've succeeded in doing that, then any topics that are on your mind are up for discussion.

Preparation

Do Your Homework

Getting an interview is one thing, performing well during one is another. What affects your interview performance more than anything else is the preparation you do beforehand. Before any interview, do your homework and learn as much as you can about the company interviewing you. Find out how strong their China business is? What is their standing in the market? What stage of growth are they in? Who are their main competitors?

Such information allows you to present and position yourself better, by speaking intelligently and insightfully about the company and industry you're dealing with. "I interview a lot of candidates who want to get into corporate finance," says Barbara Spurling, former vice president of training, development, and staffing of Asia Pacific Region for Merrill Lynch. "It's an immediate turn-off whenever someone comes into an interview completely unprepared. But the opposite is also true. It impresses me whenever a candidate can speak with some level of depth about our business or what's going on with our company."

Barbara feels that, at the very least, candidates should have a basic understanding of her company's activities in China. "With the accessibility of information over the Internet today, there's really no excuse not to be knowledgeable and prepared," she says.

Knowledge of an employer can also reflect your preparedness for taking on a new position with them. Multinational companies want people who can fit in immediately and perform with minimal start-up time. Therefore, indicate to the interviewer that you know what you're getting into, by displaying a good sense of the company's culture, their strategy, and their main products and/or services. By demonstrating an understanding of their business, you can impress upon a potential employer that you can get up to speed and add value quickly.

Researching An Employer

Many people catch sight of an interesting looking position in a newspaper or job-postings Internet site and immediately send off their resume, without even knowing much about the company receiving it. If an interview does happen, they walk in cold with little knowledge about the opportunity they are interviewing for. By researching a company beforehand, interviews proceed much more smoothly if for no other reason than there is a starting point for you to talk business. But where can company information be found?

Things You Should Know About A Company

Having some basic knowledge about a company before you interview with them is a must. At a minimum, before interviewing with a potential employer, you should find out the following information:

- *Where is the company headquartered?*
- *How long has the company been operating in China?*
- *What mainland cities does the company operate in?*
- *What are the company's worldwide and domestic annual sales?*
- *What is the company's domestic market share?*
- *What are the company's major products and services in China?*
- *Who are their major competitors?*
- *What are some of the overall trends and developments in their industry?*

If a company is a listed one, their detailed financial information and overall corporate strategy is summarized in its annual report. Reports can be obtained by calling the company directly and speaking with their public relations department. The marketing and sales departments are also usually willing to share their promotional literature on the company's products and services.

For English-language information on industry sectors and companies, the libraries at the American Chamber of Commerce, the Commercial Section of the American Institute in Shanghai and Beijing are good starting points to access statistical data and directories of businesses in China. If you need contact information for multinationals operating in China, your single, best resource would be the American Chamber of Commerce Membership Directory of the city you are targeting. The directories contain the names of executives working in just about every major multinational in the mainland. The book's price varies widely for each Chamber. For instance, the Shanghai version costs about US$90. Directories also include each person's title, phone number, fax number, and company address.

A wealth of information on prospective employers can also be found on the Internet. For example, if you're interested in working for Hewlett-Packard in China, you can visit their corporate website, which links to their China website containing information on their mainland operation. Many companies also post their worldwide job listings on their websites. You can even look up a company's products and services, corporate mission/vision statement, and recent press releases.

Whatever your methods and sources, investing some time into researching potential employers and their industry will benefit your job search by preparing you well for your interview. Such preparation allows you to feel more confident about what you may need to talk about, and lets you highlight your background more effectively to an employer. Perhaps most importantly, the information and knowledge you gain gives you a much better chance of ending up with the right company for yourself. At the very least, your efforts will help build your understanding and knowledge of the industry you are interested in.

Informational Interviews

Some candidates ask us if my firm can help them set up informational interviews with our senior management client contacts. These candidates are usually at an information gathering stage, and want to gain some insights from an established person in the industry they wish to enter. What I tell them is not to take such a formal approach in their information research. Just chasing down an executive can take a tremendous amount of time and effort. It's not that they're reluctant to speak with and help out young professionals, but they face a heavy workload and demanding schedule. And even if you do manage to arrange a meeting, it is often a short and somewhat rushed one. In truth, most senior managers are too busy to see someone just to provide them with information. If they interview someone, they want it to be for the purpose of filling a job opening.

The Average Person Knows A Lot

If it's merely helpful industry and job information that you're looking for, it can be much more easily obtained by speaking with junior and middle management professionals in your industry of interest. There is a large number of such professionals working at every level, for every multinational firm in the mainland. And because so many conversations among professionals in China revolve around business, the average person is well informed about what's going on in their company and industry. Dealing directly with clients and customers, developing and executing business strategies, and assessing competition on a daily basis, they know as well as anyone the latest developments and news in their industry.

Whenever I need company information or want to know of industry trends, I don't call upon my executive management contacts. As search consultants whose livelihoods depend on staying current with the job market, even we get most of our information through lower level management staff. For instance, if I need to know about the latest mobile phone developments in China, I'll speak with a product manager in the telecommunications industry. Or if I need a market overview of a particular consumer product industry, I'll talk to sales and marketing people who deal with customers each day.

Such contacts are easier to get a hold of, and they are willing to talk. You can also ask more sensitive questions without worrying about trying to impress them. More importantly, talking to people at the position level you seek can provide a first hand perspective of the ins and outs, and what is required to be successful at the job.

I like to invite people I'm gathering information from for lunch or drinks, at a place where we can talk informally. I let them know beforehand that the purpose of my seeing them is to pick their brain for information. They rarely decline. For most, it's flattering that you've recognized their expertise and knowledge of their industry. And altruistic motives aside, who wants to turn down a free meal?

The Kindness Of Strangers

You'll be surprised at how open people are to speak and even meet with you, particularly in the international business community. I've always found people in China very willing to share information and references. It stems from nearly everyone's universal experience of seeking help when they initially came here. They can appreciate the plight of other jobseekers. Many also found jobs through newfound contacts who provided useful information and employment leads. They've all phoned a stranger at one time, upon the recommendation of a mutual friend, to ask for help or advice.

Given China's strong networking culture, accessing people who are willing to help you out is usually just a reference or two away. Of course, any opportunity to speak with senior executives is extremely valuable and should be taken advantage of if available. However, it's more beneficial to pay them a visit when you are at the job interviewing stage, rather than just wanting their time for information that can be attained through other channels.

Multinational Employer Interview Checklist: Before You Interview, You Should:

- *Try to speak to someone in the company and/or industry that you're interviewing with.*
- *Check out the employer's website and read up on their business.*
- *Contact the employer's office for their latest annual report and company/ product brochures, to read up on their most recent developments.*
- *Practice articulating in both Chinese and English what you'd like to say about yourself and your suitability for the position.*
- *Prepare a few questions about the employer's business that you can ask during the interview.*
- *Contact employer by phone to confirm your schedule and availability.*

Avoiding The Jitters

Many candidates tell us that they get very nervous during interviews and end up not presenting themselves well to potential employers. They might say things they don't intend to say, or get caught with little or nothing to say at all. If this is the case with you, it's likely because you need to practice how to talk about yourself.

It is not the habit of most Chinese to draw attention to themselves and to highlight their accomplishments and abilities at length to others. In multinational companies, however, professionals are expected to project themselves and communicate in a forthright manner. If you can't do these things in an interview, then employers will feel it is unlikely that you'll be able to do so as an employee either.

Within most interviews, a few standard questions are typically asked. They focus on what you did in your previous job, your job responsibilities and tasks, the environment you work in, significant accomplishments, and previous educational background. To help candidates improve their interview performance, we advise them to think about who they are, what they've done, and what they'd like to do. It's surprising how little time many mainland professionals spend thinking about these things, to the point where they can talk comfortably and confidently about themselves. Once you know what you want to say about yourself, you should then practice articulating it out loud to someone. Anyone will do. It could be with friends or family members.

It's not unusual to feel uncomfortable talking about yourself. It's important, however, to be very familiar with and confident about what you're trying to sell, which is you. With a little forethought and rehearsal beforehand, you should feel much more at ease during an actual interview.

Common Topics And Questions That Multinational Employers Ask In Interviews

Although there are countless questions that could come up in any job interview, your ability to respond to the following ones should allow you to address the majority of topics and questions that multinational employers might ask.

- *What were your main responsibilities in your current/previous position?*
- *Could you describe for me/give me an example of your greatest accomplishment in your current/previous position?*
- *What about you makes you an excellent employee?*
- *What about you makes you excellent at your current/previous job as a _____?*
- *What are some of your most outstanding personal/professional attributes?*
- *How would you/your colleagues/your boss describe yourself as a person?*
- *How/from whom did you obtain your professional training?*
- *Why are you interested in this position/our company/our industry?*

Working With Search Firms

Within recent years, the greater job mobility among professionals and hiring needs of multinationals has increased the presence of executive search firms in China. Beyond their internal recruitment resources, multinationals are increasingly outsourcing hiring assignments to search firms like ours. Although there is a growing awareness that such firms can help expand their job search for desirable positions with leading companies, mainland professionals should better understand how to work with this valuable resource.

The executive search industry also goes by the name of "headhunting," for its aggressive approach to seeking out potential employees for company clients. Search consultants are known as headhunters. Their primary role is to identify, pre-screen, and submit a selection of candidates to clients, in response to job requirements that they receive. Job interviews are then arranged with candidates that are of interest to the client.

If you receive a call from a search consultant, they may or may not have a specific position in mind for you. If they do, most likely you will only be one of many candidates they are contacting. It is standard practice for search consultants not to reveal a client's identity during their initial contact with you. They should, however, be able to provide you with position details and responsibilities. But until they are convinced of your interest in the opportunity, they will not release to you their client's company name.

Once a search consultant determines that your background is of interest, they will arrange to meet with you to further discuss your experience and interests. Be as candid as possible by sharing with them the same type of information you would with a prospective employer. Many candidates can be guarded about revealing themselves with a search consultant they've just met. However, the more a consultant knows about you and your career objectives, the better they will be able to match you to an appropriate position. After all, it is also in their keen interest to successfully place you in a position with a client.

Because of their close client relationships, search firms are also an important intermediary between you and the company. The consultant can provide detailed information on job requirements, company culture, and management style, as well as assist you in the negotiation of compensation. Their insight can also help gage a company's interest in you.

Misleading or giving inaccurate information to a search consultant can be highly detrimental. Search firms put their integrity and reputation on the line with clients by speaking on your behalf. Such misrepresentation can be extremely harmful to all parties involved. And although you are free to send your resume to several search firms at once, as a professional courtesy you should inform the consultants you are working with of your job search activities, particularly in the case where two firms want to introduce you to the same client. Such a situation creates a controversial situation for everyone.

If after submitting your resume there are no positions that match your background, your information will be kept on file until a suitable opportunity arises. Some candidates will call and follow-up often to ask whether a position has appeared for them. In such cases, we assure the candidate that if we're not contacting them, it's because we haven't yet come across an appropriate job match. However, they can phone whenever they like to update us with their employment status, or just want to touch base with us for a job market update.

Most companies use search firms to help them identify professionals with previous work experience, rather than for fresh university graduates or entry level hires. This has to do with the premium service fee that companies must pay search firms for their involvement in successful placements. For example, the positions my company works on typically requires candidates to have at least four years of solid work experience.

As the use of executive search firms by multinationals becomes more widespread in China, upwardly mobile professionals would do well to leave their resumes on file with a few top search firms serving their industry. Knowing of opportunities in the job market not only helps you have a better understanding of your competitive and career situation, it also keeps you abreast of industry trends. Overall, it is to your benefit to establish a good working relationship with a search consultant. It can lead to attractive job opportunities that respond to your career interests.

Tips For Various Job Seekers
University Undergraduates
Unfortunately, directing resources towards undergraduate recruiting and entry-level positions is usually a lesser priority for multinational firms. As a result, you're likely to find few on-campus job placement channels. This doesn't mean, however, that there aren't plenty of attractive entry-level positions available within leading multinationals. However, finding such jobs for undergraduates is based almost entirely on self-effort.

Internships
Summer job internships with multinational firms present a good news, bad news scenario. The bad news is that summer internships are not much of a concept with companies in China. Most multinational operations have not yet developed structured internship programs. The hiring emphasis is on full-time positions, which are difficult

and time-consuming enough. In addition, many managers barely have time to supervise full-time staff, let alone a temporary intern.

The good news is that there is a tremendous need for interns by most companies. Short-handed managers can use smart, motivated interns who can support projects, compile and organize information, or conduct market research. The concept of employing summer interns does make sense. The need and willingness by international managers are there. The problem is that most simply don't have the time to arrange and hire for such short-time positions.

Therefore, if you want a summer internship, it's up to you to be proactive and to initiate contact with these managers and create the opportunity. I've seen many students secure internships with companies who weren't even looking to hire an intern. They did it by gaining the attention of busy managers and selling the skills and benefits they could provide. They made a case for what they could do to make the manager's job easier. Typically, the emphasis was not on compensation. In some cases, students were merely looking to cover expenses, in return for a chance to gain as much exposure and experience as possible.

Personal Travelogue

Summer Internship

Within my own MBA summer job search experience, I first tried to secure an internship in Taipei from the U.S. through on-campus interviews. The companies hiring for Asia-based internships, however, were few. In addition, those firms I spoke with were not looking for someone like myself with poor Chinese language skills and no regional work experience. They sought students with stronger local backgrounds who were more likely to return to Taiwan after graduation.

Beyond these few campus interviews, I then began writing directly to branch offices in Taipei. I mailed over 30 letters, but received only a handful of lukewarm responses. Those who wrote back either expressed a lack of interest or politely informed me that my resume would be kept on file.

Without another option, I flew to Taipei over my spring break. After arriving, I arranged some interviews through a third party contact who knew marketing managers at several consumer product companies. Not one manager I spoke with had an idea to hire me for an internship before I walked into their office. Nearly every conversation began with the remark: "Rick said that I should talk to you, what's on your mind?" During these meetings, I spoke of my analytical skills, marketing sense, and unbridled eagerness. Most managers were only able to offer me advice, or another contact or potential job lead to follow up on. All were receptive.

During a meeting at Johnson & Johnson, the marketing director happened to have recently launched a new shampoo product that was showing disappointing sales results. There was some market research data that she wanted to reevaluate. She felt that there might be some important, overlooked information that could help improve the positioning of the product. Noting my quantitative background as an engineer, she thought I might be a good person to re-analyze the data. During our second meeting, she made me an offer. I accepted. I was paid modestly, but was provided with free housing.

Over the summer, I re-examined the market research data and did, in fact, discover some additional findings. I used the information to develop a tighter positioning strategy and new ad campaign for the product. By the end of the summer, my boss even asked me to consider staying in Taipei and forego the second year of my MBA program to oversee the product's re-launch. Based on this experience, I'm a firm believer in the need and interest of multinational managers in Greater China to hire summer interns.

Working for Free

During my MBA program twelve years ago, I wanted to find a summer internship in Taiwan in the marketing field I was interested in. At the time, I had limited Mandarin skills, was unfamiliar with Taipei's business environment, and lacked hands-on marketing experience. With no interest from companies initially, I sought advice from a friend who owned his own company and had hired many young staff over the years. When I told him I had nearly run out of ideas on how to get companies interested in me, his advice was somewhat startling. He said, "Have you ever thought of approaching an employer and offering to work for them for free?"

When he said this, I thought it was the most ridiculous advice I had ever heard. As he continued, however, I began to see the value of such an approach. I was confident in my abilities. But what I lacked and wanted was experience. All I needed was an opportunity to prove myself.

It's an approach I have since recommended to many students looking for part-time work or summer internships. For an employer, an offer by a bright, young person to work free of charge is a low risk proposition with few downsides. Many managers in China are busier than they care to be, and are understaffed. And although they may have many projects that could use help, their budgets are frequently limited.

From your side, working for free gives you a chance to gain experience and inside knowledge in an industry that might interest you later on. Just the exposure to full-time professionals alone can be invaluable towards your pursuit of future career opportunities.

In addition, a work-for-free arrangement allows you to continue to pursue other opportunities, since you can arrange your work hours in a flexible manner. Job searches may take months, but do not occupy every hour of the day. Rather than spending the time waiting idly for employer responses, why not be productive and have something to show for by working on a part-time basis.

The offer to work for free, however, may not be automatically attractive to an employer. It still requires them to invest the time in supervising you, and to take a chance that you will perform beneficially. When proposing the idea to an employer, identify and suggest possible areas where you believe you can add value. These can include projects that relate to market research, database development, translation work, or marketing support.

The most important factor in a work-for-free arrangement is that the benefits and work being done are attractive to both the employer and yourself. The approach has helped several young graduates I know to gain experience that later helped them find a full-time position in the same field. Beyond the hands-on exposure, they also attained a better understanding of the industry they sought to pursue. Ultimately, they were able to talk more confidently about their suitability for a job and the strengths they could offer an employer. From a multinational employer's point of view, the initiative and commitment of this type of person is impressive.

Mid-career Professionals: Switching Careers
Be Realistic And Patient

Many mid-career mainland professionals approach us to express their desire to change industries. They might have entered their current industry expecting something quite different, or joined a company for no other reason than its well-recognized name. At some point, however, they come to the realization that they are not very interested in the job or line of business they are in.

If you feel there is another industry that you are well suited for and can be successful in, be flexible and consider taking a temporary step back so you can move two steps forward later on.

If you feel there is another industry that you are well suited for and can be successful in, you may need to be realistic and initially take a slightly lower title or position of responsibility in order to show a new employer what you can do. Be flexible and consider taking a temporary step back so you can move two steps forward later on. After all, there's an initial learning curve that you must go up. In addition, there is a risk factor to your potential employer in giving you the chance. If you can lower that risk factor, then there's a greater likelihood that they'll give you the opportunity you seek to prove yourself.

If you have confidence in your abilities, show a little patience in reaching your goal in the new industry you wish to enter. Demonstrate your performance. If you're as good as you think you are, you should be able to quickly prove your value. In a reasonable amount of time, the level of responsibility you are accustomed to should be restored.

Don't Overlook Fundamental Skills

One woman was upset because she was almost 30 years old and was still working as a secretary. She wanted to change jobs and redesign her career, but had no idea what else she was suited for. She was a politics major in university. After graduation, she became a teacher. Because her English was quite good, she later became a secretary in a foreign company.

In China, I have met many former secretaries and administrative assistants who have outstanding skills and potential to pursue a wide range of careers. Through their administrative duties, they have had close, frequent exposure to experienced senior managers, many with international backgrounds. If they've worked in a multinational firm, their English is typically very good. They are usually highly professional. They also have a good understanding of how a corporation operates. These skills are all very attractive to employers and provide a strong foundation for any professional wishing to develop a long-term career in an international company.

Because of their strong organizational, coordination, and communication skills, in particular, I've seen many switch to and excel in account servicing positions in industries such as advertising, public relations, media, executive search, consumer products, and marketing communications. These industries constantly seek staff who are good communicators and who work well with clients.

As an example, my company has hired several executive search consultants who began their careers in administrative roles for international companies. For many who start their careers as secretaries in China, your future job opportunities and career prospects are very promising. Your well-rounded qualifications, training, and experience make you highly desirable.

Factors Beyond Your Control

Attaining your ideal job may not happen immediately. Timing alone can dictate when the right job opportunity may present itself. The finance industry in Hong Kong is a prime example. In late 1992, China began allowing mainland companies and enterprises to be listed on international stock markets. From 1992 until about the fall of 1994, investment banks hired almost indiscriminately in anticipation of the upcoming underwriting activity to take place. If you had any type of quantitative skills as an engineer, accountant, or graduating MBA and the ability to speak even a little Mandarin, you were likely to have your pick of several offers.

Unfortunately, China's financial markets under performed relative to expectations. Banks began to down-size from the aggressive hiring that took place just months earlier. By the beginning of 1995, even candidates with finance industry experience had difficulty finding a job.

Markets, industries, and companies in China are subject to rollercoaster cycles that change quickly and unpredictably. Such factors are beyond your control. Nevertheless, based on nearly every forecast that projects continued growth for China's economy, good opportunities will eventually appear. And hopefully it will happen sooner rather than later. The important thing for you is to be prepared when these opportunities do present themselves.

Be Pro-Active

At some point during your efforts to land a position in an international company, it can feel like you're spinning your wheels without getting anywhere. Although there are increasing employment resources to tap into and a growing number of attractive job openings available in multinational companies, persistence is required.

Many multinational job postings in China aren't even advertised. Your ability to know about and pursue them comes from knowing the right people. For someone working full-time and with limited time to search for a new job, this is a difficult reality. To improve your chances, you need to understand the hiring emphasis and mentality of multinational companies, utilize the resources available to you, and have a proactive approach to accessing positions and winning over decision-makers. By following the examples of those who have successfully made the entry into a multinational firm, you can increase your own likelihood of working within one.

Personal Travelogue

Creating Your Own Opportunities

Perhaps the biggest break that helped bring me to Asia was a random meeting with someone I had never met before. I was trying to get a summer internship during the first year of my MBA program and decided to fly to Taipei during my spring break. I had never been to Taipei before, didn't know a single person there, and had no interviews lined up. Undeterred, my plan was to arrive in Taipei and cold call like a maniac. As soon as I landed, I bought a directory of U.S. companies in Taiwan and began making phone calls. After five days, I had managed to arrange a couple of interviews, but nothing that came close to resulting in a summer job. I had no solid leads and was due to fly back in four days. I was beginning to foresee the impending disaster. "Damn it, I've come all the way, and now I'm going to go home empty handed," was the anxious thought pulsing through my head.

By chance, I happened to look in my wallet and notice a phone number written on a scrap of paper. The number was from a classmate, who suggested that I call her sister's husband in Taipei. At the time I was given the number, I thought nothing of it. I just stuffed it in my pocket. In an act of desperation, I called him.

The person invited me to his office. We talked a little about ourselves first. It was very casual. I remembered that he was from San Francisco, so I brought up the 49ers. He perked up. When I saw that, I began pouring on the sports talk. Having lived in Taipei for over three years, he was out of date with the latest news on his favorite team. We began to really hit it off. Although I was enjoying our talk, my main thought throughout our conversation was: "Pleeeease, like me, like me, help me, help me!"

After thirty minutes, he looked at me and asked, "so what can I do for you?" I told him about my interest in finding a marketing job in a consumer products company. "And by the way," I added sheepishly, "I should probably let you know that I don't speak much Mandarin, have never worked in the region, and have never worked in a marketing position before. Do you think you can help me?"

He paused for several moments to take in my weak credentials and to ponder my situation. He then reached for his Rolodex and began pulling out name cards. While I sat in front of him, he proceeded to call up his marketing friends at Pepsi, Johnson & Johnson, Quaker, Nestle, Procter & Gamble, and Coca-Cola. Within another thirty minutes I had seven meetings set up over the next two days. I ended up interviewing with and accepting a summer internship with Johnson & Johnson the day before I left.

Certainly, I was extremely fortunate this guy was willing to help me. Yet, I've heard many similar stories where a new acquaintance was able to provide a key introduction that eventually led to something. I call this, benefiting through "the kindness of strangers." Situations similar to mine happen all the time in Greater China.

Part IV

Once You're There

Chapter 11 Your Professional Development: Insights And Guidance

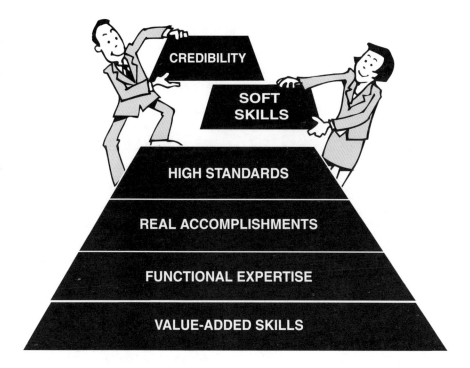

CREDIBILITY

SOFT SKILLS

HIGH STANDARDS

REAL ACCOMPLISHMENTS

FUNCTIONAL EXPERTISE

VALUE-ADDED SKILLS

Take Responsibility For Your Career

We receive numerous emails each week from mainland professionals who feel under-utilized or short of challenges in their job. Or they remain stuck at middle management, unable to get ahead, while their colleagues advance. They wonder what others are doing to get promoted that they aren't? My response to those facing such situations is that they have to take greater responsibility for their own professional development. Many are simply not proactive enough in seeking opportunities and managing their career.

As has been emphasized, exposure to international managers and business situations is key to gaining the right skills to get ahead in a multinational company. Some are fortunate enough to have the opportunity to study or work overseas. Others may work for a manager or in a company that is looking after their career development. However, the majority of mainland professionals find themselves in situations where they lack the resources and access to the opportunities they desire.

If the opportunities you need are not being given to you, then you have to try to create them for yourself. For instance, if you are producing quality work that your company is satisfied with, then don't be afraid to approach your management to give you additional projects and assignments that are of interest to you. It may not be the case that they are reluctant to do so. They might just think you are already challenged enough by the work being given to you, or they might be pre-occupied or unaware that you can handle a greater workload or more responsibility.

Sometimes, you have to be patient and give your management a chance. Work may be slow because of natural business cycles or company restructuring. However, if you find that you are constantly waiting around for challenging projects to be assigned to you, then you need to initiate steps to find a better situation for yourself. Likewise, if you feel that it's the case that management is not taking an interest in your career development, or that they are just not capable of offering the growth opportunities you need, then you should seek out a situation that will.

The great thing about the business environment in China today is the abundance of excellent jobs that are available in multinational companies for qualified individuals. For example, for information technology (IT) companies and their clients, speed and execution in the development, implementation, and use of technology is essential. For those with the combination of information technology and business backgrounds, there are plenty of challenging positions to be found. However, you can't just wait around for such opportunities to be handed to you. They're out there. But it's up to you to go after the ones that will best suit your professional needs and ambitions.

Michael Chu: Build Your Value

Personal History: 33 years old. Born in Beijing, raised in Shanghai
Parents: Mom is from Ninbo, Zhejiang Province. Dad from Henan
                     Province
Education: Bachelor of Law degree from the Institute of International
                     Relations in Beijing. Major in International Journalism.

Michael Chu is a director for a leading international public relations agency in Beijing. One of the things he enjoys talking about most is the topic of management and managing staff. He confesses that about 70% of his time these days is spent on people management issues, that includes hiring, mentoring, and developing his staff.

He often tells them to design their own career path. "Once you have an

Michael during a recent trip to Inner China

objective, you have to pull the pieces together to make it happen," he says. "In many instances, your company can help you to grow and achieve your goals. However, sometimes they can't. In some situations, nobody can do it for you but yourself. You have to recognize those situations and find ways to grow yourself."

Michael has been pulling the pieces together throughout his own career. He is someone who has grown through the rank and file into his current management role. Early in his career, he envisioned himself as a future GM for an international company operating in China. Coming out of university, however, he did not possess the skills he needed to be successful in his profession (Michael spent his first four years in the hospitality industry). For instance, he did not develop his English fluency in a classroom. Rather, he learned it while speaking on-the-job each day. He also developed his problem solving approach and international perspective by reading whatever he could get his hands on, and by traveling abroad whenever he could.

Today, when asked what his two main strengths are as a public relations professional, Michael identifies his English language ability and open-minded manner of thinking. He knows how to critically analyze situations and come up with creative solutions. He can also express himself clearly and comfortably to international clients. These capabilities are particularly relevant in his industry, where professionals are distinguished by their ability to respond to crisis situations.

"Many people focus too much on their weaknesses, and not enough on their strengths. It's your strengths that are what you will be most successful competing with. For me, I spend about 70% of my energy trying to improve on and use my advantages, and about 30% work on my weaknesses."

Today, Michael's greatest challenges as a manager are making sure that his staff have room to grow and identifying short-term goals that each one can achieve. He has seen many young mainland professionals too eager to negotiate for greater responsibility. "The company gives it to them, and they end up failing. They just aren't ready yet," says Michael. "It's a real setback for their career. Before you negotiate, you need to make sure that you are playing with the right chips."

His advice to mainland professionals is to always make sure to do the basic things right. "Consistently doing a job well puts you in a strong position to grow," emphasizes Michael. "Good managers notice a lot. They can see the consistency in your performance and the way you approach even minor tasks. When you get to a point where you are needed by the company, you are in a much better position to say what you want to say and do what you want to do. The key is to make yourself a strong professional. Once you build your value, then the responsibilities, titles, and money, will follow."

Build Fundamental Skills

Young mainland professionals always tell us they are looking to get into a management role, where they will be given them greater responsibilities. They are so anxious to become somebody. For too many, however, their approach to attaining such an opportunity is to change jobs to a company that is willing to give them what they want, even before they have mastered the skills or proven themselves in their current position. It's a short-sighted approach that can be damaging to your career development in the long run.

If you want to build a strong career, you need to be realistic and mature about what it will take for you to succeed. Undoubtedly, there are many attractive jobs out there. However, you have to ask yourself if you are ready for such opportunities, even if they present themselves to you. It's more important to identify the fundamental skills you need and work towards building those capabilities.

> *Undoubtedly, there are many attractive jobs out there. However, you have to ask yourself if you are ready for such opportunities, even if they present themselves to you.*

In my own situation, it took me five years to come out to Asia from the U.S. I was 25 years old when I first got the idea to work in Greater China. At that time, however, I really didn't have the skills to attain a position in Asia that would give me the best chance to develop my career in the manner I sought. I knew this. Although I had some work experience, it was not as relevant to the new environment I sought to enter. I didn't speak Mandarin back then, nor did I have a basic understanding of industries, markets, or business practices in the region.

Rather than just sit still, however, I began taking Chinese lessons while I continued to work in the U.S. I also talked to as many people and read as many books as I could about doing business in Greater China. I even returned to school for an MBA in international business. By the time I graduated, I was much better qualified and more attractive to companies operating in Greater China. One eventually made me an offer and transferred me out here.

I'm not saying that it will take five years to achieve your goal, or that you need an MBA to get where you want to go. But early in your career, you should build up a solid foundation of basic skills first. Most practical for those wishing to enter a multinational today are English training and an understanding of international-caliber business practices. It's hard work developing these on your own without the benefit of going abroad, but with the availability of information and access to learning these days, helpful resources are much more accessible than ever before.

Finding good opportunities in China today is not at all difficult, especially with the countless number of jobs posted on the Internet. The far greater challenge is whether you can qualify for an outstanding position when it is presented to you.

Personal Travelogue

Bold Enough, But Not Yet Good Enough

As a first-year MBA student, I had my heart set on working over the summer in Greater China. Unfortunately, only a handful of firms came to my campus to recruit for overseas internship positions. I remember receiving an invitation to meet with one consumer products company. At the bottom of my resume I had written the ambiguous words, "proficient in Mandarin."

Anticipating a test of my language skills during the interview, I practiced my Mandarin responses, drawing from my vast first-year level of training. In the end, my conversation with the native Mandarin-speaking company representative ended up being rather short:

Me:	Ni hao. Wo de mingzi shi Larry Wang.	(Hi, my name is Larry Wang)
P&G Interviewer:	Ni hao. Ni jintian hao bu hao	(Hello. How are you today?)
Me:	Wo hen hao. Nin ne?	(I'm fine. And you?)
P&G Interviewer	Wo ye bu cuo.	(I'm also fine)
Me:	Hen hao, ...	(That's nice) ... silence

With only one year of Mandarin under my belt, it was not easy being a captivating conversationalist. Yet, on we chatted.

P&G Interviewer:	Ni de fumu[*] cong na li lai de[**]?	(Where are your parents from)
Me:	Uhhhhh, ... dui bu qi, ni keyi bu keyi zai shuo yi ci?	(huh?!?)
P&G Interviewer:	Okay, ... well, let's see, ... that's good, ... ummmm, ... so, how 'bout them Yankees!	

---

[*]   I later learned that "fu mu" was a more colloquial term for mother and father. In Chinese class, we had always used "baba" and "mama." No wonder I was thrown off.

[**]   I had also never heard the expression "cong na li lai de" before. I had learned the textbook way, "ni cong nar lai de." Clearly, an honest mistake.

The interview brought to light a particularly harsh reality. I was still at a point where I was nearly hopeless at speaking Mandarin with a native speaker, or with anyone not reciting lines from a first-year Chinese textbook. Add to that my heavy western accent and I don't think I was fooling anyone into thinking I could conduct business in Chinese. I guess that's why my campus interviews for Greater China internship positions lasted only the few minutes they did. The only thing I could do was to keep working at improving my Mandarin. Eventually, I realized that I would have to immerse myself in a Chinese speaking environment if I was to develop any real fluency.

Diversify Your Business Skills

Although they are currently in comfortable positions or with good companies, quite a few mainland professionals that I speak with are worried about remaining competitive in the job market. For example, a female candidate who majored in computer science expressed her concern about the high-speed evolution of technology that would effectively obsolete the software techniques she was currently trying to master. She was afraid that her hard-learned skills would soon be outdated. My recommendation was that she extend her professional capabilities beyond pure programming.

With technology so much a part of today's world, an abundance of positions exists with information technology companies that are selling products and providing services to businesses and individuals. These companies seek staff who can provide technical consulting, pre-sales and post-sales support, and project management to customers. To perform in these roles, a strong understanding of technology is needed. In addition, however, they also require strong communications skills, an understanding of business situations, and an ability to analyze problems and implement technology-based solutions.

Many technology professionals in China fail to look beyond their computer, to notice a rapidly changing business world that seeks well-rounded professionals. Strong general business skills, in combination with good technical knowledge, is a winning combination in today's job marketplace. Such business skills allow you to apply your technology background across a greater range of products, projects, and job functions, even as new technologies evolve and come to market.

The same is true for professionals in other functional areas and industries as well. Beyond your core expertise and competencies, develop broader capabilities that will give you greater job flexibility and longevity in your career.

Work Smarter, Not Harder

There is a saying in the west that goes; work smarter, not harder. Multinational managers I talk to all recognize mainland professionals as hard workers. They are able to imitate quickly and repeat what they are taught. However, on the down side, these same managers do not view many of their mainland staff as being very efficient in their work. They feel that many are not fully switched on when performing a task, in a way where they are trying to figure out how they can do things easier and quicker.

"Many of my staff don't use the resources available to them, or know how to improve on the way they are doing things," says the account services director of an international advertising agency. "As a result, their overall effectiveness is poor. They're willing to work long hours, but not necessarily with the intensity and mental involvement it takes to do the job faster and better. They'll eventually reach the objective, but they take much more time to do it than what they should."

Be a Thinker, Not Just a Doer

A promotion from a staff level to management position in a multinational organization implies an ability to transition from being a work doer, to a thinker and problem solver. However, many multinational managers feel that too many of their mainland employees prefer to just execute and be instructed. Of course, that's an easy way to approach any job. And more than likely you can get by in this way. But you can't expect to move into higher management roles by putting this type of effort into your work. This is particularly so in multinational companies that require managers to respond to fast-changing situations and handle complex business issues.

Brenda Chung is the director of operations for the top foreign residence housing estate in Suzhou. The Singapore-owned estate contains over 400 homes and services over 600 expatriates and Chinese residents. Within her responsibilities, she runs the company's marketing and customer service department. Because their clients are mostly foreigners, her mainland staff must speak good English. However, their greatest hurdle is their limited international exposure and, therefore, understanding of the expectations of the foreign residents.

Therefore, Brenda places particular value on employees with a curiosity and willingness to really learn their business. She underlines the importance of understanding what you are doing, and not just following instructions. She finds that many of her staff go about their jobs without purpose. She'll teach them how to handle a situation, and they'll do it. But if another situation occurs that is slightly different, she'll have to teach them all over again. It's because they don't bother to think about things any deeper than what they have to.

"My best staff is a customer service manager who questions me back," says Brenda. "Whenever she's given an assignment, she'll always ask, "how come we do it this way? It's not to challenge me, but to try to understand more completely the reasons behind the service we provide, as well as the attitudes and expectations of our residents. While other staff must be painstakingly taught how to deal with every customer service instance that arises, she is able to come up with ideas, figure out new situations, and then respond appropriately to them. From the company's point of view, that's an invaluable quality that we look for when promoting staff to management roles."

Understand And Share Corporate Values

For international companies, attractive management candidates are ones who are able to understand and develop the values of the company within the organization. Sharon Dong sees her role as a manager very clearly. She is the managing director for Octagon Prism's Shanghai office, an international events management company. "The most important aspect of my job is to make sure that the corporate philosophy and business approach that differentiates our company are passed on smoothly to our staff. Our industry is highly competitive. Each company has its strong reputation and expertise. And pricing among major players is similar. It is, therefore, crucial for our people to understand and believe in our company's own unique qualities and successes. They need to understand how these are directly linked to our ability to grow our mainland business. And that, ultimately, when the pie gets

"The most important aspect of my job is to make sure that the corporate philosophy and business approach that differentiates our company are passed on smoothly to our staff."

bigger for the organization, their pie gets bigger too, through greater career opportunities."

The Way To Better Opportunities

Many foreigners working in China will tell you that there is a big difference between how internationally trained managers and mainland managers perceive the sharing of knowledge and information. While most mainland managers see the sharing of information with colleagues as a threat to themselves, most international managers view it as a means to bring them greater opportunities.

When Gene Dorris first began his corporate training company in Shanghai last year, he was the only one among his staff who was certified to deliver the company's core training course. Within six months, however, he had made sure that every consultant in his company became certified to deliver the course training as well. When he told this to a mainland friend, the friend asked him, "Why did you do that? Now everyone can do what you can do. You've lost power."

Gene looked at him in disagreement and responded, "No I haven't. I've gained power. Our capabilities are much greater now and my company is in a much better position to succeed today than six months ago."

Brenda Chung's situation also shows the benefit of training and developing her staff. "Later this year my company will relocate me to Shanghai to start up and run our new business development office there. I would never have been given that chance if in my previous role as director of operations, my staff were not any good and if our board of directors did not feel that they could handle our customer service issues in Suzhou without my presence. Transferring my knowledge to them was the key to my receiving the current opportunity that I'm being given. Hey, if you don't empty the cup of its coffee, then nobody can fill it with champagne."

Differentiate Your Value

Perhaps the key to being promoted into management positions is to demonstrate the outstanding qualities you have to offer that go above and beyond what the next person has to offer. Many mainland professionals are good performers, but they don't necessarily differentiate their skills and value to the organization, their management, or to colleagues. Mainlanders at manager levels in a multinational company can receive a great deal of scrutiny in the eyes of your mainland colleagues. "I tell our newly promoted managers that the best way to gain the respect of others in the company is to show that you can do certain things better than they can," says John Chen, the general manager of a U.S. electronics manufacturer in Shanghai. "That may include your ability to develop staff, resolve issues, formulate strategies, identify opportunities, or provide industry or market expertise. By demonstrating such abilities, it becomes clear to everyone why you are in a position of higher responsibility."

Get Involved

The fear of speaking up to management is an obstacle for many mainland professionals. But holding back and avoiding involvement not only hurts you, it can also hurt the organization you are a part of. Nandani Lynton tells the story of an off-site management training exercise that she attended where participants were broken up into teams. Each team was given a problem, and a time limit to determine the solution.

"On our team were several foreign and regional Chinese managers," recalls Nandani. "There was also a young mainland woman who was more junior than the others. During the game, whenever she was asked for her opinion or thoughts, she would say, "I don't know," or "I'm not sure." She acted in a very traditionally courteous and modest way. Near the end of the time limit though, she finally spoke up to say that she thought we were pursuing the problem the wrong way. She went on to explain a different approach, which she felt we should have taken. Her answer was exactly correct! But because she held back during most of the meeting, we lost the game."

"During the time she was keeping her thoughts to herself, I'm sure she felt she was being polite and that there were no consequences to result from that. But by not participating and sharing her ideas with the rest of us, she deprived the whole team of a much better outcome. It's the same with multinational organizations and the objectives they seek. They want managers and staff who will involve themselves to their fullest in the company's activities, to increase the likelihood of gaining the best result."

It is true that many mainlanders are naturally shy relative to foreigners who are accustomed to expressing themselves more openly and freely. A withdrawn personality or fear of offending someone can always be used as an excuse though. However, the underlying reason why many do not speak out usually stems from a lack of confidence. The best way to overcome that feeling is to build yourself into a strong professional, based on your possession of greater knowledge and strong business skills.

Seek Out Mentors

Before joining a multinational public relations firm, Jessie Wang worked for five years in a state-owned enterprise. She differentiates the management's attitude towards internal communication and staff development within the two environments. "Managers of SOEs don't TALK TO staff. Usually, they TALK DOWN to them," she points out. "Trust is hard to establish, and mentoring seldom exists. Managers do not encourage self-development and open communication because it can be threatening to them. Instead, they like employees who are quiet and who always look busy. For example, if you get your work done quickly and are seen with extra time on your hands, instead of being viewed as a strong performer and receiving encouragement, you're accused of not working hard enough."

If there is one factor that can benefit your career, it is having a good mentor. For young mainland professionals, mentors can be like career counselors and teachers who can provide you with invaluable guidance, information, and general business sense. They have seen and experienced a lot in their career, and possess the type of knowledge that you can benefit greatly from. Most importantly, they can broaden your perspective and give you the insight you need to make good decisions in developing your career. Mentors can help you when contemplating a new job or position, or if you just need feedback on an idea that you have in mind. They can also assist you in figuring out how to handle office politics or a tough business situation.

Approaching someone to act as your mentor is not as difficult as you might think. Although busy, many managers are quite willing to be mentors simply because they can appreciate young people who are earnest and ambitious in their careers, much like they were earlier in their life. Many enjoy recounting and sharing their experiences and successes, particularly if it can be helpful to others.

Most important is to identify mentors on the basis of your ability to communicate openly and develop a rapport with them.

The mentors you identify can come from anywhere. They don't even have to be from your company. Most important is to identify mentors on the basis of your ability to communicate openly and develop a rapport with them. They should be someone whom you respect and trust. Asking someone mainly on the basis of their title can provide minimal benefits, particularly if that person doesn't really have the time or a genuine interest in helping you.

June Pu has worked for four different bosses over the years and has rotated through various functions in her company. She feels fortunate that each one has been an excellent supervisor. "I've learned a great deal from each of them, and value every one as a mentor and friend," says June. "Even today, I seek them out whenever I need input on a problem or difficult decision."

You should keep in mind that the managers that you might approach as mentors are likely facing daily pressures and demanding schedules. Therefore, be considerate of their time. Until you've established a good, comfortable relationship, seek out your mentor only on matters of importance. Make it as convenient for them to meet with you as possible. When you do meet, be prepared with what it is that you'd like to talk about.

You should also use discretion when dealing with your mentor. For example, speaking openly and frequently with a high profile mentor within the same company can cause unwanted politics or jealousy among those around you. While working in her previous company, one candidate drew the attention of the company's general manager, who became interested in assisting her career. The general manager tried to help her by instructing her supervisor to give her certain opportunities, and to make sure the rest of the office supported her. This not only strained her relationship with her boss, but when her co-workers found out, they grew alienated from her as well.

Finally, although asking for business contacts or references can provide a great benefit to you, use good judgement regarding a mentor's willingness to help you in this area. Mentors may be willing to open doors for you, but they don't want to feel that this is the emphasis of your relationship with them. They can feel cautious and resentful if asked to yield personal contacts, without yet feeling comfortable with you. This shouldn't be a problem, however, if you have built a close relationship with them. Best to approach mentor relationships in a professional, more formal manner initially. In the best instances, they will develop over time to be more personal in nature.

Relationships with experienced, knowledgeable business people whom you can turn to for advice can make all the difference in making the right choices at critical moments in your career. There are people I know who maintain and call on a network of mentors often when facing crucial situations. It's funny, but they usually seem to make good, sound career decisions for themselves.

Protect Your Professionalism And Credibility

Developing a strong strategic outlook, becoming a good problem solver, or managing people well are not the kind of professional capabilities that are acquired over night. Rather, they occur through an ongoing, day-to-day process of practice and improvement. Each person's potential and time frame to display excellence in these areas will vary. Good managers know this and are realistic and supportive with regards to what a person needs to attain such skills.

Similarly, gaining new customers, setting up new channels, and delivering services and goods also takes time to make happen and are subject to many unpredictable market and business factors. As an example, in our experience of providing recruitment services, we often face situations where it is extremely difficult to produce the result that the client is seeking, given the shortage of top quality management talent in the region.

However, we've always found hiring managers and human resources personnel to be quite reasonable about the limitations and obstacles we may face. As a result, despite the inability to sometimes deliver excellent candidates within a short time frame, we are able to maintain our good standing with clients by consistently demonstrating our professionalism and responsiveness to them.

Whether reporting to the management in your company, or doing a job for a customer or client, there are certain things that, as long as they're done, can help you maintain the confidence and support of those you are dealing with. For our company, doing these things can make the difference between whether a client continues to respond and work with us, or not. The key is not to let our credibility and our client's trust and confidence in our professionalism be broken. There are really only a few key instances where this may occur. By avoiding those instances, we are able to maintain excellent relationships with our clients, despite the fact that we may not always be able to deliver exactly what they want, when they want it.

Set The Right Expectations

Perhaps the most damaging situation to your credibility that you can create is setting an expectation for someone and getting them excited, only to have the result fall far short. People don't like to be disappointed. The best way to avoid doing that is to always be as accurate and complete as you can in what you communicate to others. For instance, we lose the confidence of a client if we describe a candidate as having excellent work experience, but the client does not discover that in the interview. Or if we say that a person is highly interested in their company, but in the interview they do not appear so.

If you're not sure of a situation, explain why and let the other party know that you'd like a little more time to assess it. People can respect that. It shows honesty and even thoroughness on your part, attractive qualities to anyone who is dealing with you. Overall, there's no need or benefit to making promises that you do not feel you can meet.

It's not about creating excuses to cover your tracks, should a situation that you feared arise. Rather, it's about utilizing your judgment and knowledge of that situation so as to not mislead others and waste their time.

Follow-through On What You Tell Others

If you say that you'll get back to someone by a certain time, you should do so. Even if you don't have the result or answer they want yet, let them know where you are in the process. It gives them assurance that you're working on their issue and have them in mind. Otherwise, they develop the impression that you are not on top of their case, or are not providing the type of professionalism and service they want. The client won't know which is the case unless they hear from you.

It only takes a minute or two to pick up the phone or send a quick email to update someone on a situation. Our clients don't mind so much that we haven't introduced candidates to them by a certain deadline, or if we ask for a little more time. Mainly, they want to understand the situation and be updated, so they can determine whether they should pursue another course of action to attain the result they need. What many don't like, and won't tolerate long, is being ignored.

Avoid Surprises

Our clients hate being caught by surprise, particularly finding out bad news or situations that they feel we should have known about and informed them about earlier. As a recruiter, we always need to be up to date on and communicate well the key factors that impact the likelihood of a candidate joining our client, such as a candidate's interest level, expectations, and job search situation. Discovering something entirely unexpected in these areas at a later stage in the interview process is a huge disappointment to a client and bomb dropped on our credibility to provide value-added service to them. To avoid such let downs, our consultants must determine and present this critical information up front in each case.

In the business world, particularly when you're dealing with high caliber people and situations, your credibility and professionalism mean everything. Guarding how others perceive those qualities of yours should be among your highest priorities as a professional. And beyond just clients and your management, you should demonstrate that same consideration and professionalism with others in our company as well.

Maximize Your Ability To Learn
Think Of Yourself As A Student

Frank Chen is one of the top marketing professionals in the region. Over a 15+ year career, he has worked for major international consumer products companies, including American Express, Nike, and Unilever. Still, Frank talks about himself in this way. "As much as I know I'm a coach and teacher at this stage in my career, I always think of myself as a student first," says Frank. "There are so many things I don't know and am still learning. When you think in that way, you become less enamored with what you think you know, and more focused on what you should know."

"As much as I know I'm a coach and teacher at this stage in my career, I always think of myself as a student first."

Having a grounded perspective that allows you to learn and grow is important for anyone. This is especially true for professionals early in their career who don't yet have the depth of exposure to many business situations. In my own company, new employees are expected to get up to speed and contribute quickly. Typically, they enter our company without previous experience in our industry. When they first come on board, I provide them with a few tips that I feel are important for their personal and professional development.

Be Humble

Personally, I believe that it's unproductive to spend time thinking about how good you are. What purpose does it serve? What benefit does it provide to you? When a person spends a lot of time thinking that they're great or successful, they get disappointed when others don't tell them that too. I don't spend one second thinking about how good I am or what a good job I've done. However, I do constantly think about how I can do things better, and what else I should be doing to get to where I want to go.

I also never seek accolades. What others say about me has little impact on my self-esteem. Most important is to know what a good job is and what isn't, and to know if you're doing one or not. If you have high standards for yourself, then you will likely meet the expectations of others as well.

Having Pride vs. Being Prideful

Having pride is great. All exceptional people have it. For myself, I have pride in my family lineage and in being Chinese. But being prideful is an entirely different thing, and it can be harmful. Prideful people do not take criticism well. They're defensive. They are overly sensitive to what others say about them. As a result, they're not good listeners or as observant as they should be. Having too much pride, or being prideful, can be a great equalizer. It can make very smart people dumb, by inhibiting their ability to learn, to seek and take on advice, and to recognize their mistakes. It's important to separate having pride and being prideful, and to know to what degree you are of each.

From a manager's perspective, the most difficult employee to deal with is a prideful person who doesn't know what they don't know. To begin with, they are unable to recognize their weaknesses and lack a depth of understanding about many things. Often, they are not even aware of what it is that they need to learn or improve upon. Unfortunately, because they are also prideful, their stubborness makes it extremely difficult for them to develop and improve when you try to teach them. As a manager, you quickly reach a point where you only have so much time and energy to deal with such a person.

Be Self-Critical

In speaking with highly successful people, they often tell you that they are their own harshest critic. Similarly, you should be your own toughest critic. In my own case, many things we try as a company are different or are considered fairly original in our industry. When first introduced, our ideas may be criticized and exposed to failure. But no matter what anyone says about me and what we do, I've usually said them to myself already. I do not believe anyone is more critical with me than the way I am with myself. The benefit of that is that I am able to listen to outside opinions without reacting defensively. Such comments can be very helpful in improving your performance, if you are able to accept them.

Be A Sponge

When it comes to learning, there are people who are like a piece of silk, not too absorbent. Instead, you need to be like a sponge. If you can, you'll be able to develop and learn much faster. When I was 27 years old, I went through a sort of blossoming in my career. At the time, I wanted to raise my level of performance as a professional and transition from being good, to becoming exceptional at whatever I was doing. To do this, I reassessed everything about myself. It didn't matter that I had an Ivy League degree or a promising career track in a Fortune 500 company. In order to improve myself, I told myself that I didn't know much. It's because I wanted desperately to elevate my standards. The first step to achieving that was to open my mind and figure out what it was I needed to learn and do. With that perspective, it was easier for me to seek out and listen to the insights and viewpoints of others.

Recognize What High Standards Are

I know of people who claim to be perfectionists. They claim to have high standards and consider the work they do to be of high quality. Unfortunately, their standards and quality of work are, in reality, not that high relative to those that are truly considered excellent. It's always good to set high standards for yourself, but make sure you are able to recognize what high standards really are. The best way to do this is to talk to and observe professionals more experienced than yourself, whom you respect and whom you wish to emulate. Take note of their level of performance as a determinant for

It's always good to set high standards for yourself, but make sure you are able to recognize what high standards really are. The best way to do this is to talk to and observe professionals more experienced than yourself, whom you respect and whom you wish to emulate.

success. This will help you set standards worth aiming for that will elevate your own professional skills and capabilities.

Don't Take Yourself So Seriously

No matter what happens, try to have the capacity to look honestly and openly, and to even laugh, at yourself. My partners and I have made numerous mistakes during the course of building our company. Some errors have even been embarrassingly naive. But through it all, we have always had a great time together. We always try to keep in mind that perhaps this is what we need to go through in order to learn the lessons to ultimately succeed. We have no problem saying out loud to each other, "we suck!", and laugh about it. Then, we move on, by applying what we've learned, and trying harder to get it right the next time.

Seek The Truth

Everything I've mentioned is all tied up into one thing, knowing yourself well. This means knowing what you are and aren't, what you can and can't do, what you have to offer and what you need to learn. Knowing these things allow you to be more humble, more honest with yourself, and more focused. In turn, they will help you to develop faster and more completely as a person. In the end, I believe you will have greater patience, a deeper understanding of situations, and genuine confidence in your abilities as a professional.

Seek Learning Situations

Susan Pattis identifies having a strong EQ, or emotional quotient, as an important quality for professionals who wish to perform at a high level. Those considered to have a high EQ are in tune with their surroundings and are able to "get the point" in any encounter. They have an excellent ability to read and, therefore, to respond to situations. They are also good observers. Typically, they have excellent people and communications skills. As a result, they are able to present and handle themselves consistently in a mature, appropriate manner.

A strong EQ is highly related to a person's exposure, which gives them a better understanding and awareness of situations. Susan advises her staff to get out and "do anything" outside of work that will help them develop a greater understanding of the world. This can be done by simply interacting with others, observing situations, taking classes, reading books, or even watching movies. She stresses the importance of creating a habit of continually developing your knowledge base. For instance, Susan makes it a point to read 20 pages of a book each night, no matter how busy or tired she is.

She also encourages her staff to meet as many people as they can and to build a diverse network of professional and personal relationships. "I don't mean relationships of *guanxi*," clarifies Susan. "But one's with people whom you share a feeling of mutual trust and interest in each other. These are people you can learn from, and who will add value to your life."

Finally, Susan encourages those who have the chance to take opportunities to travel and see the outside world. Until most mainlanders are able to experience other international cultures and perspectives, they will have a difficult time really knowing and understanding them. She believes that many of those who do well in multinational companies have developed their intuition for handling new situations they encounter, by increasing their awareness and exposure to other countries and their people. "The more different types of situations you face, the more mature it helps make you," Susan emphasizes. "That's a fundamental, common quality that many successful multinational executives have."

Insights And Development Can Come From Anywhere

Learning something about yourself, about business, or about what it takes to succeed in life can come from anything you do. Rose Ngai recalls a slow period in the mainland's economic situation, and not being able to find a full-time job with a multinational or Chinese company after graduating from her masters program. Instead of sitting at home though, she made every effort to keep herself busy. "During that time, I took all sorts of low-level or temporary jobs," she laughs. "I worked in a small convenience store, sold ice cream, sold Chinese arts and crafts products, and did research. Looking back now, many of the skills and understanding I gained in those jobs were very helpful in the business situations I faced later as a professional. That one year also gave me time to think about what I wanted to do with my life and those jobs I did helped me mature as a person."

For many of us, some of our greatest and most valuable attributes, such as perseverance, resourcefulness, perspective, and maturity are developed during seemingly unspectacular or average times. You shouldn't underestimate or overlook what each situation you encounter can teach you. Such experiences can have tremendous application to your long-term development and future success as a professional.

Have Some Patience

One piece of advice for mainland professionals that was repeated by nearly every executive I spoke with was clear and simple. Don't be so greedy. Rather, be patient and demonstrate real achievements before moving on, as opposed to trying to get ahead on credentials or because of short-lived, opportunistic situations. Too many young professionals today are eager for higher titles and the responsibility to make decisions way before they are ready. They believe that every twelve months they should get a promotion. Part of the reason is the pressure they feel from peers, and their fear of lagging behind.

In one example, a young accountant wrote to describe the working environment of his current company. His boss was providing him with opportunities that were benefiting his development. He was considering changing jobs, however, because he felt that the caliber of his colleagues was extremely high. This was causing him to feel competition and creating a situation where he was always facing one challenge after another.

I told the accountant that I felt that the situation he was in was a very fortunate one. Unless he was finding himself no longer growing, I recommended that he stay where he was for now and continue to learn as much as he could. Actually, most mainland professionals find themselves in the exact opposite situation. They feel stuck in a position or company that lacks the caliber and exposure that they wish to have access to. They seek an environment where they can not only set goals, but where they feel that they actually have a chance of achieving them. This is exactly what he had. The competition he faced from colleagues was challenging him to deliver exceptional performance. The high standards in his company would help him develop excellent capabilities that would benefit his career over the long-term.

For professionals in similar situations, move on only if an opportunity offers you substantial advantages that your current company cannot, or if you feel certain you are ready to test what you have learned in another job situation. To reduce the pressure on yourself, try not to focus solely on attaining one goal after another. Such a process is never ending. Instead, learn to enjoy the developments and achievements you are experiencing. After all, most of our time and effort in life is spent on the road traveled, rather than at a final destination point. As a result, you should try not to overlook the enjoyment of the journey you're on.

Ying Han: Success The Old-fashioned Way — By Earning It

Personal History: *Born and raised in Beijing.*
Parents: *Father was a Chief Engineer of an SOE in the chemical industry. Mom an accountant.*
Education: *B.S. in Accounting from Xiaman University*

Ying Han was introduced to me by a top Internet investment analyst in Hong Kong. The analyst described Ying as one of the most impressive mainland executives he has met. During my first meeting with her, it was clear why. In listening to her talk, it was apparent that she loved the field of accounting and finance. And as a result, she was very good at it.

But her career began in a modest manner. After returning from the countryside at age 25, she found a job as a worker doing car repairs for a state-owned enterprise. Most significant about this first job though, was that it exposed her to the field of finance for the first time. In addition to repairing cars, she was given the chance to handle the company's book keeping. Hungry to learn, she also spent this time learning English on her own, from the radio and TV.

Ying at a recent presentation awards ceremony in Hong Kong

She then began working at the headquarters of China Offshore Oil Company in 1978, one of the first mainland companies to deal extensively with international investors and commercial banks. "At that time, few mainland Chinese had experience dealing with foreigners," recalls Ying. "I was included on the business development team because of my English abilities. For the next three years as a financial analyst, I worked on oil projects of US$500 million in average size, and interfacing with top professionals from Exxon, Mobil, and Chase Manhattan."

The oil company also sponsored her education at Xiaman University, which was famous for its accounting department. It was the first university to offer western accounting courses.

Ying first became aware of Hewlett Packard China in 1988, when she passed a building one day and saw a job advertisement on its front door for a senior accountant opening. Although she applied and interviewed for it, she was told that she was too qualified for the position. It wasn't until a year later that HP contacted her again and made her an offer for an accounting supervisor position that was opened. The timing was right, and she accepted.

HP was the perfect environment for Ying to demonstrate her excellence. She took the opportunity she had to improve the financial processes within the company. "One area that I was able to have an impact on was getting local banks involved in distributing the company's payroll," says Ying. "It was a practice that was not common, or even known at the time. It was contributions like this that gave me the feeling that I could do significant things and be recognized for them."

Over the next ten years, Ying would also hold positions as a finance manager, business administration manager, and a business development director, before becoming chief financial controller. She chose each role based on how the new experience could round out her own business skills and expand her understanding of the company's business.

When the opportunity at AsiaInfo came up, Ying faced a tough decision. There were still many opportunities for her at HP. However, while China might be years or even decades behind the west in many industries, it was possible for a Chinese company like AsiaInfo to be at the same level or even a major worldwide player in the Internet. It was an opportunity she couldn't turn her back on. Today, as AsiaInfo's chief financial officer, Ying particularly likes the financial management opportunities she has to improve the company's overall efficiency, drive results, and support top management.

From her experience, Ying shares this advice for approaching a career. "Before 30 years old, you should get into the best opportunity you can to learn best business practices and to see the whole picture in the functional area and the industry you're a part of," she says. "Fundamentally, you need to understand the game you're playing and what you need to know and do to become successful at it. You should also use this time to develop yourself as a first line manager. Focus on gaining management skills and on testing yourself to see if you can lead people. By the time you're 30, you should then have the experience and knowledge in your field to be able to set and pursue your long-term career goals. At least, that's how it's happened for me."

Developing Yourself As A Future Executive Today

Developing the capabilities and skills to someday be a high-flying manager or corporate executive is something that doesn't happen over night. It begins today. It should start right now. Your development for performing in such future roles is tied into everything you do and each situation you encounter along the way. So beyond just concentrating on learning a job function early in your career, you will receive much greater benefits by also being aware of and working on certain habits and practices that will help you perform within progressively higher levels of responsibility.

What Characteristics Do You Most Identify With A Strong Executive?

Before focusing your efforts on the things you need to do to prepare yourself for future management, however, you should first form a good understanding of what it takes to be a successful executive. You can begin by asking yourself what are the most outstanding qualities of a strong manager or business leader. Of course, the individual styles and strengths of each successful executive are quite varied. Likewise, the list of qualities will vary for each person, depending on your own personal strengths and the characteristics that you most admire and wish to emulate.

When I was in my mid-20s, as I was contemplating what it would take for me to evolve into a capable manager, I spent some time defining what kind of business leader I wanted to be. The characteristics I chose were mostly selected from those managers I looked up to and was fortunate to know. In my case, I've always identified with, and continue to emphasize today, the following four leadership attributes:

Excellent Communicator

People have always told me that I am a good one-on-one communicator. I believe it's because I take a genuine personal interest in the people I speak with. But I've also always recognized the importance of presentation skills and effective writing skills in business. Being able to address audiences and communicate concepts or sell ideas is very common at an executive level, whether in a meeting room, client presentation, or media opportunity. Therefore, since early in my career, I have always sought opportunities and practiced the skill of standing up and speaking in front of others.

In addition, there have been many occasions over the years where my success in achieving a result has been related to a memo or letter I wrote that was able to communicate clearly and simply the issues, and what needed to be done. I've trained myself over the years to write in a concise, impactful manner, by always being sure to get quickly to the point and highlighting those points effectively.

Force of Personality

I also refer to this as your professional charisma, or the ability to lead others through your personality, intelligence, intensity, focus, and/or even humor. I believe many successful business leaders are people whom others are drawn to and want to follow. It is a powerful quality to be able to captivate others to some degree, whether it is in selling an idea, motivating or leading a team, or building relationships.

Warm and Generous

This one may not be on everyone's list, but it is one that I've always felt is important in the type of business leader that I wish to be. As in all aspects of life, most of us respect and respond to those who are generous with others. Fundamentally, I believe that kindness is often rewarded and an effective approach to draw others to your objectives, rather than by merely imposing your goals on them. This holds true in business as well

I know some people who are generally warm and generous. However, within their company or in a business situation, they are often stiff, formal, or overly professional. I believe that if you can convey the natural, positive qualities of your persona, then people will perceive you as approachable and cooperative, which are healthy characteristics for any business leader. In addition, your ability to solicit the desired response and effort from those you deal with will more likely occur, regardless of how strict or demanding your management style may be.

But it's not just how you treat those above you, such as your boss or people who may be important to you, but how you treat others at your level, or even below you as well. I believe one of the most flattering comments you can receive is when people feel that you are someone who treats the tea lady in the same way you treat your boss. That's a person who will be able to solicit loyalty, trust, and goodwill among those they lead.

Tremendous Business Instincts and Insight

This one is the most essential and hardest to attain, since it is primarily developed over time and through your exposure to numerous hands-on situations. It's not difficult to learn and understand any one task quickly. But developing the depth of knowledge and insight so you can make excellent judgment calls in related situations is something that happens over repeated encounters in a variety of scenarios. In other words, it is gained with experience.

Beyond these executive and leadership characteristics that are personal to me, there are many others that can be quickly identified. They may include having tremendous drive or aggressiveness, the ability to learn quickly, or the ability to manage resources. Your awareness of such qualities and how they apply to you is a first step. Whichever ones you feel are most important, identifying them early on should help you develop over time an effective, comfortable management style that will serve you well as you encounter increasingly higher level situations throughout your career.

Essential Capabilities Of Successful Executives

Beyond a suitable definition of what a successful business leader is, you should also understand what capabilities one must possess in order to handle the situations that an executive must face each day. You can then start working on developing those capabilities for yourself. In my experience, the following ones apply to just about anyone who handles a great deal of responsibility:

Ability To Juggle Many Balls In The Air At Once

Senior managers are always juggling many objectives, decisions, and situations that come their way all at once. They must think about the immediate term, but always consider the medium and long-term as well. They must handle matters in a way where all three are being taken care of at once.

In addition, it's not good enough just to be able to do a task well. Anyone can do any one task well. But as an executive, it is necessary to do many things well, and all at the same time. Therefore, if you are expecting to handle a heavy, diverse load of responsibilities in the future, you better learn how to be very good at multi-tasking.

Fast

In order to manage so much responsibility all at once, you also better be fast. You must be able to learn fast, do things fast, make decisions fast, and handle situations fast. If you recognize this early in your career, and you are someone who is able to consistently learn tasks well, then your next step is to train yourself to do them well, and with speed!

Take Pressure

The higher you go, the more responsibilities, decisions, and pressures are placed upon your shoulders. Therefore, you need to be able to handle the weight of it all. If early in your career, you feel the pressure from just focusing on one main task, then think how you'll feel when you must bear the weight of five, six, or ten equally major ones.

To handle such pressure, day after day, it is important to develop and maintain a perspective. That means, a perspective on the importance, priority, and sense of urgency of each task. By sorting these things out, you can focus your attention on the most critical areas, and spare yourself from other areas that can needlessly sap your energy. Your career should be viewed as a long race. Pace yourself and parcel your energy. If you're always finding yourself sprinting, then you may burn out and never make the finish line.

Great Decision Maker

Aside from working fast, it is perhaps most critical in an executive role to make good decisions. As a senior manager, it's all about getting results. Effort doesn't count. Poor decisions waste a tremendous amount of time, energy, and resources, and can make the difference between whether you ultimately succeed or fail in the challenges you take on. Therefore, it's crucial that you put your effort into those areas that will get results. That begins with knowing how to make good decisions that consistently identify what those areas are.

By identifying the capabilities that you'll need later on early in your career, you can engrain them into your daily approach to doing things. Developing the skills to become a strong executive does not need to happen sequentially, step-by-step as you advance in your career. Rather, they should be practiced continuously and applied to every situation you face. By working on these capabilities right now and each day, as you are also learning the basics of an industry or job function, you will be much better prepared later on as you to move into positions of higher responsibility.

Perhaps most significantly, understanding the importance of such capabilities allows you to pursue everything you do with a greater sense of purpose. For instance, whenever I learn a new skill, it is not good enough that I am able to just perform that skill. Instead, I constantly challenge myself to see if next time I can you do it faster and/or more effectively. Or if I can do it fast and effectively while at the same time juggling several other significant tasks. Because ultimately, that's the type of scenario that high level executives regularly face.

Raising Your Standards

I meet many young mainland professionals who are well trained. They are extremely capable. Their academic qualifications and knowledge of business concepts are quite good. When you give them a task to perform, they are able to understand it quickly and can eventually produce the desired result. In doing so, however, they view this achievement as a level of performance that deserves to be recognized and calls for their career advancement.

From an executive's perspective and standard of performance, however, real achievement is reflected in one's ability to sustain performance, both consistently and at a high level. For most people, it is not too difficult to perform any task once. However, are there higher standards that you should achieve to demonstrate your real capability and expertise in performing that task? For instance, are you able to:

- perform it in a shorter amount of time than you do now? How much faster?
- perform it simultaneously, at twice, three, or five times the volume of what you do now?
- recommend ways to improve the efficiency or result that the task produces?
- effectively train others to be successful at this task?
- manage a team of people to be successful at this task?

These are the achievement standards that potential managers are measured by, and that stand out to experienced executives as indications of one's depth and ability to perform in a particular area. They are also the levels of capability that attract attention and give cause to consider a person for promotion and further opportunities.

Part V

What Else You Should Know

Chapter 12   Most Often Asked Questions

If you're contemplating working for a multinational company and have some basic, but important questions on your mind, then this could be the most helpful chapter in the book. Based on countless candidate interviews, Q&A sessions, phone and email inquiries, these are some of the most often asked questions that mainland professionals have on their minds regarding getting a job and developing their career in a multinational company.

1) How Good Does My English Have To Be?

The bottom line on English language skills almost goes without saying - the more the better. Without diminishing its critical importance, however, near native proficiency is not always necessary. It depends on the situation and who you're dealing with. It's more about communicating effectively.

Some professions and industries do not necessarily require English language fluency. For instance, in sales positions, where government ministries or local business entities are your primary clients, the use of English is seldom required. Another example is within programming and software development positions, where the interaction with outside parties and management is limited.

Typically, however, the higher one advances, the more critical the need for English fluency. Within multinational companies, senior managers (i.e. director level or higher) in China must deal frequently with regional operations, high-level international clients, and other senior managers.

The simple advice we give mainland professionals is that if your English skills are weak, work on them. For most, it is the single biggest obstacle to gaining the type of international exposure and professional manner they desire. More than anything else, it will help you achieve your goal of joining a leading multinational company and participating at a management level once you're there.

Most mainlanders I meet actually read and write English at a fairly competent level. However, when it comes to speaking and listening comprehension, there is a large drop off in their capabilities. Although I do not claim to be a language expert, I have had the experience of learning a second language myself. If you are committed to learning English, I believe you must first come to terms with certain realities.

The first is that you have to expose yourself to as many situations where you can actively practice your speaking and listening skills. Such opportunities are available to you every day, through social functions, language classes, or encounters with English speakers whom you can practice with. English videos, movies, karoake, and TV programs can also help you expand your vocabulary and improve your listening comprehension.

The next is that you will likely feel very uncomfortable when placing yourself within situations that force you to use your English. Many mainlanders I meet have studied for years. They diligently read books and take classes. Yet, their spoken English is poor. It's because they rarely use it in real situations. They feel too embarrassed.

Of course, you're going to feel embarrassed. But that will never change unless you reach a level where you develop some confidence and start enjoying using your English. When I first moved to Taipei, I spoke little Mandarin. But whenever I was with colleagues and friends, they only spoke to one another in Mandarin. It took a great amount of concentration just to follow simple conversations, and most of the time I could only understand half of what was being said. I often felt stupid, out of place, and embarrassed. However, I knew that it was the only way I was going to learn and improve.

Finally, learning English is a lifetime pursuit that requires a daily effort. It's difficult to have confidence in the beginning when you know your level of performance is not very high. However, those successful at learning a second language are persistent and dedicated. They try to be "dense." Meaning, they disregard what others think and ignore any embarrassment they may feel. They find a way to enjoy the learning process and not be so sensitive to their mistakes. The bottom-line is that learning English is not easy. To succeed though, you have to adopt a mindset and approach that allows you to make progress in the best way possible.

Personal Travelogue

Jumping In With Both Feet, ... And Drowning!

On my first day at Wang Laboratories' Taipei office, the general manager arranged a meeting to introduce me to the management team. After he made a few brief comments, I was called upon to tell my new local colleagues something about myself. As I stood up, I sensed their uneasiness at having to deal with a native English speaker. But I had a surprise for them. I was no home office-sent expat, totally unfamiliar with the Chinese language and culture. I was ready. I had been practicing this moment for weeks, you could even say years.

In my well-rehearsed Mandarin, I spoke for several minutes about my upbringing, educational background, family history, and even favorite hobbies. My two years of classroom Mandarin study were seeing their crowning glory. My recitation was like a dramatic reading from Shakespeare. I was pleased and proud of my performance. When I sat down, I felt vindicated for the countless hours of hard work I had endured. I anticipated their response, thunderous applause and awestruck admiration. Perhaps even a standing ovation. I was certain I had impressed everyone.

And there it was, a sigh of relief on the faces around me. A visible feeling of relaxation permeated the room upon the realization that I was one of them. Now it was their turn. One by one, each manager stood and described their responsibilities. A flood of high-speed Mandarin, no, make that super high speed Mandarin, came spewing forth.

From outside appearances, I listened intently to each speaker. I nodded occasionally to acknowledge what was being said. I laughed heartily with everyone else when witty remarks were made. I even guffawed and slapped my knee one time, nearly doubled over with laughter when one colleague made a lighthearted joke directed at me.

Inside my head, however, I was in a panic! What the hell were they saying?!? More to the point, what language were they speaking?!? I wasn't picking up any of it! This was nothing like the Mandarin on my first-year lesson tapes. They were speaking three times as fast!

I felt a warm, prickly sensation on my neck and moving down my back. Perhaps the only sign of my discomfort came from my rapidly tapping index finger that pounded the conference table. It was a reflex movement, my finger trying to hit the pause button on a tape recorder, as it had done hundreds of times before. Only this time there was no response. I couldn't stop it!

What a nightmare. Here I was, in the midst of my professional peers and unable to understand a thing being said. What to do? Speak up and admit stupidity. Lose total face? With each passing second, the option to jump up and say, "I'm sorry, I haven't understood a word any of you have said. I'm just wasting your time," became more difficult to do. I pressed on and listened with greater intent. Perhaps I needed to concentrate harder. Great idea, it only made me feel more incompetent and fraudulent. It was the first of many instances where I had that feeling.

2) How Important Is An MBA?

During the career development presentations I do for mainland professional audiences, inevitably, it's never long before someone asks, "do you think it's worth it to get an MBA?" To this question, my initial response is always, "it depends on the reason that you want an MBA in the first place?"

Often, people will say that they just feel they need one, as if an MBA degree will allow them to magically accelerate their advance into management ranks. Without a doubt, it has provided this type of benefit for many. However, for those seeking an MBA just for the sake of having one, the end result often leaves them little farther ahead after the two years (and an investment of tens of thousands of RMB) than if they had continued working during that same period of time.

To assess whether an MBA is "worth" it or not, you need to identify clearly your personal and career objectives. Start by determining what stage you're at in your career development. Then ask, what it is that you expect to get out of an MBA program?

What an MBA represents and can deliver is incredibly diverse, with each person's MBA experience being very different. Many pursue it to acquire fundamental business training (i.e. finance, marketing, operations, etc.) that they may not be able to acquire in their job, or that they have not studied before. Some use their MBA as a chance to make a career change, or to learn more about other industries. And many simply seek an MBA to boost their confidence. After all, an MBA does gain attention in professional circles (and it certainly doesn't hurt to mention it when meeting the parents of a significant other). Often, it gives people the "edge," or advantage, that they're looking for.

What an MBA represents and can deliver is incredibly diverse, with each person's MBA experience being very different.

Beyond identifying your objectives, you should also evaluate the quality of the MBA program(s) you apply to and its ability to deliver what you seek. For instance, with U.S. schools, the environment and quality of MBA programs vary greatly. There are many smaller, more obscure programs that are little known and that are not recognized even in the U.S. In these cases, the value of your two-year degree often amounts to little more than an expensive piece of paper that provides minimal real benefit to your career.

As much as the program itself, whether an MBA delivers the benefits you seek depends on your own focus and effort in the program. For instance, what you learn outside the classroom is often more valuable than what you learn inside them. Being active in student organizations, interacting with diverse and talented classmates, and meeting and interviewing with company representatives can also offer chances to enhance your skills and understanding of business and management.

Interestingly, multinational companies and hiring managers place less emphasis on an MBA in China than in the U.S. It's because, above all else, the mainland's business environment is an entrepreneurial, hands-on one, where practical experience counts the most. The newness of many business practices, industries, and markets means that there is usually no one to tell you how to get a job done or attain a result. MBA courses and textbooks cannot tell you how to negotiate deals, introduce services to clients unfamiliar with the value of what you're offering, or convince distributors to represent your products in the mainland. Some managers I speak with are even wary of MBAs. Their perception is that MBA graduates are too theoretical and office-oriented, and unwilling to get down and dirty to perform less glamorous, yet necessary tasks.

Nancy Xu is one of those multinational managers who believes that mainland MBAs need to be more realistic about their value within China's labor market. As the human resources director for a major electronics manufacturer, she meets quite a few MBAs in her recruiting efforts for the company. Having an MBA herself, she knows what can and can't be learned in a business school program. "MBAs in China need to develop themselves step-by-step, just like any other successful professionals," says Nancy. "Many of the ones I've interviewed are very strong at presenting themselves, but their insights are empty. When you talk to them, you don't really sense their solidness below the surface. For multinational employers like us, the bottom-line is that we'll pay for experience and skill sets, but not for education."

In certain career tracks like consulting and investment banking, however, an MBA is needed for career advancement into senior levels, similar to how it is abroad. One professional had four years of manufacturing industry experience prior to joining a U.S. consulting firm in Shanghai as an analyst. After three years with the firm, she's considering her next step. She feels the pressure to go back for an MBA. "There is an unwritten rule in top consulting firms that you can't move up without one," she says. "The choice is to either go to business school or change industries."

When considering the value of an MBA to your career, look at your existing skills, both professional and personal, and determine if an MBA will help you add capabilities relevant to your future success. If you're looking at an MBA as a ticket to get you into a multinational firm, it's not a must by any means. Certainly, there are many highly successful non-MBAs working in international companies who have shown that excellent opportunities can be obtained, without having to go back to school.

Ultimately, an MBA program is merely an environment of professional training resources that offers excellent opportunities to better oneself. As I've often said, an

MBA never hurt anyone. It's a credential better to have than not to have. The exposure that a top business school program offers is without question. But how you maximize its benefits can vary dramatically. The value of an MBA is greatest for those with clear objectives in mind up front, who are ready to take advantage of what a good program has to offer.

International vs. Mainland MBA

During one presentation, a student wanted to know if Mainland China-educated MBAs were as competitive with foreign-educated ones in the eyes of multinational managers. In truth, the overseas-educated MBAs do receive better access to world-best practices and resources, as well as greater exposure to the business world beyond China.

However, the great equalizer in China is that what counts most is how well an individual performs. Career advancement in multinational companies is based on results. Despite the advantages that they are exposed to, many overseas MBAs come back without the right perspective to immediately be effective in China's local business environment. They may be out of touch with the market, relative to local MBAs who have continued to build those relationships and base of experience.

As with mainland-educated MBAs, the success of foreign-educated MBAs is not guaranteed. However, if you do have the chance to study abroad, by all means, take it. Not just for the MBA degree itself, but for how living in another country can enlighten and broaden your view of both yourself and the outside world.

3) How Long Of A Commitment Do Companies Expect?

During the interview process, an interviewer will try to sense your commitment to working with their company. The reality is that, for most of us, it's difficult to know whether or not we'll remain with a particular company beyond even two years. There are just too many unknowns that can have an affect on your situation. Will China's economy continue to expand? Will the company you choose continue to perform well enough to offer the opportunities you seek? Will you even be successful in or like the company and the industry it's a part of? Both the macro picture and your own situation change too rapidly and dramatically each year to make such long- term predictions.

Most hiring managers do not expect you to state an intention of staying five years or more. What they are trying to gage is your maturity and commitment towards developing your career in their business. They want to sense how well thought out and serious you are in working for them. Are you looking for a long-term career opportunity, or just your next job?

From your side, you are not obligated to predict what you might be doing five years from now. People leave companies for all sorts of reasons that can't be envisioned. Many leave much sooner than planned because the work was not suited for them. They may not have gotten along with their boss. Or, perhaps the position wasn't challenging enough.

Working for a company is a two-way street. There are no guarantees in terms of what both sides will deliver. Whether a person stays with a company for a long time depends not only on the value an employee delivers to that company, but also to what degree a company can offer benefits to that employee (i.e. career development, good working environment, competitive salary, etc.).

In truth, what says more about your likelihood to stay with a company is not what you can say about your future, but what you've done in the past. Experienced managers and human resources personnel can easily spot "jumpers," or candidates who hop around to whatever industry or company is currently hot. Without the indication of previous job stability, future claims carry little weight.

Conversely, candidates who are long-term oriented and career-minded are also easy to identify. These candidates have shown tangible achievements in the positions they have held and real growth in their career development. They can discuss business situations and scenarios they've been involved in at a deeper, more knowledgeable level. For candidates with such a track record, their claims of pursuing a long-term opportunity are much more credible to prospective employers.

4) What Can I Do To Break A Long-term Employment Contract I Have Signed?

In order to know the restrictions for leaving a job before the period of time you have signed on for, you need to review the employment contract terms to determine what the penalty is. Beyond the strict legal implications, however, you can also pursue your termination of employment through more personal ways. If you have a good relationship with your manager, you should talk to him and see if you can get him to understand your situation. I don't believe many companies wish to continue employing someone against their will. If your management knows of your situation and desire to leave, they may even want to help you to do what's right for you. Or they might feel that your lack of desire to continue in your position is not a good situation for the company either, and would willingly let you go, without penalty.

Corporate policies and contracts aside, at the end of the day you are still dealing with people. As such, each situation can be handled in its own unique manner, according to the circumstances and the relationships that exist between the individual parties involved. Every company is bound to have its employment policies that act in the best interest of the organization. However, you won't know how strict your management is in enforcing these areas until you ask.

My long-term advice is to avoid signing employment contracts in the future that require you to guarantee your employment for over two years. In today's job market, with companies and industries changing so dramatically from year to year, it is not realistic to predict what a situation will look like several years down the road, for either a company or its employees.

5) How Do I Explain To An Interviewer Why I Have Changed Jobs So Often?

Job hopping, of course, is severely looked down upon by employers. A resume with several positions over a short time span can reflect a person's tendency to be unfocussed, impatient, or undedicated. However, a "messy" resume can happen to anyone. You may have taken a job that, in retrospect, you shouldn't have. This happens two or three times and before you know it, you appear to be someone who seemingly switches jobs on impulse or at the first sign of difficulty.

There are instances where a candidate's "jumpy" resume initially turned me off. But face-to-face, the person reflected a professionalism and dedication to pursue a stable career track. Usually, the candidate fully realized that their job history looked bad. They were merely seeking a suitable opportunity where they could prove that they had a mature career outlook and ability to stick to one position.

If you believe that your reasons for job switching are credible, then be straightforward in talking about them during an interview. Don't try to overlook the problem area. Don't make excuses. An interviewer's concern over your job stability will be on his mind until answered. Address the issue and then move past it as quickly as possible, instead of letting it linger with the interviewer. Your willingness to talk about it up front lets them sense that you have nothing to hide. When I meet a candidate with a suspect background, I am naturally curious as to why the frequent job moves occurred. Typically, I'll have a question or two to raise. If I'm satisfied with the answer(s), I'll move on.

One candidate I met had the misfortune of changing jobs three times within a two-year period. And she was looking once again. When I told her that the frequency of her moves may be a problem with potential employers, she acknowledged that she was fully aware when leaving each job that it might raise questions about her dedication. Rather than make excuses though, she admitted that changing jobs in each case was a decision she dreaded, but felt she had little choice in making. She let me know that she would respond to any questions I may have.

When I asked her to comment on the moves, she was able to give me valid reasons that I could relate to. They included unforeseen management changes, significant company financial difficulties, and misrepresentation of position responsibilities. She was entirely believable. She was so sincere and straightforward that I ended up empathizing with her and her past situations.

At that point, she asked if she could tell me about her background and job interests. Beyond those initial few minutes, that's exactly what we talked about for the remaining hour. It became apparent that she was a mature person and hard worker. She was able to impress me with what she knew and what she had done, despite the movement in her previous positions.

There are times in your career when poor decisions may have been made, or things have not turned out as planned. Such instances are unfortunate, but understandable. In such cases, step back and take a look at how you might view someone in a similar situation. If your story sounds believable to you, then there's no need to hide or excuse it. Address it so you and your interviewer can move on to what you both are most interested in talking about, which is your job skills and your ability to perform within the opportunity at hand.

6) Should I Quit My Job And Just Look For My Next Position?

Although it's difficult to recommend such an extreme course of action to anybody, I've seen it work out for many people who have taken the plunge and left their job to look for a new position. Those who have successfully done it generally fall into two categories.

The first type were taking a fairly safe, calculated risk. They conducted some initial research to identify potential positions and to speak with others working in the companies they were targeting. During this time, they were able to assess the job market and their chances for finding employment. They concluded that good opportunities were available to them. Landing a position was only a matter of time, once they could put a concentrated effort into their search. They usually had one or more substantial job leads in progress that needed just a little more time to be realized.

The second type were just totally committed to the idea of changing jobs. Moving on to another company was their clear interest. They no longer saw any benefit or advantages to staying where they were. As a result, they did not feel there was any big risk or sacrifice in leaving their company. They took a long-term perspective and saw each day in their current job as another day they could be developing their career in a more beneficial manner elsewhere.

For professionals used to working and receiving a regular salary, however, unemployment can be a heavy psychological and financial strain. Quitting your job before securing a new one is not a decision anyone can make for you. Not everyone's situation is suited for such a bold move. You have to weigh your own personal situation, abilities, and objectives. There are no guarantees, but with the right preparation and perspective, such a move can work out favorably.

7) Should I Work For A Small Or Large Company?

Although working for a large, well-known company can be attractive for its name recognition and training resources, smaller firms can also be an excellent career choice if selecting the right situation. Smaller companies tend to have a more relaxed, flexible work atmosphere. Whereas large corporations can laden employees with reports and 'busy work," the work within smaller operations tend to be bottom-line oriented and have direct relevance to the firm's success. With limited resources, they operate in a highly practical manner.

In addition, the exposure and degree of responsibility in smaller companies are usually quite broad and very hands-on, since management needs to make full use of every employee. As a result, employees are typically required to be versatile, with the ability to handle a variety of tasks. Additionally, because employees and management are often in situations where they are working closely together, good performance is more readily recognized.

Leveraging small company work experience at a later point in your career, however, can sometimes be difficult. Perhaps the greatest drawback of smaller businesses is the lack of formal training they provide. If you decide to seek a corporate position at a later time, hiring managers may wonder about the quality and scope of your work experience. Being unfamiliar with your company, they have little way to evaluate and gage the caliber of your work and work environment.

Many smaller businesses also tend to work with smaller clients and business cases. As a result, the exposure you seek may not be as broad or high level. I've set up interviews for many candidates who have worked for start-up companies. They've shown impressive resourcefulness, ingenuity, and performance within their previous job. Yet when placed into a larger, more structured corporate environment, they do not have a good feel for what they know or where they stand professionally. When interviewing with large multinationals, they lack confidence or are sometimes intimidated by the more formal manner and surroundings.

Therefore, when considering a smaller company opportunity, it is important to look at the professional exposure that the firm's business will offer you. Does their business require a professional approach (i.e. strategic planning, marketing, business analysis, etc.), or does their business succeed on relationships or sheer volume of activity? Evaluate the company's management team. What are their professional backgrounds? Have their careers developed within corporate settings, or strictly entrepreneurial ones?

You should also find out about the management structure of the company. How will you be supervised? Although flexibility and independence can be great, a close, mentor relationship that provides regular feedback is more beneficial in the long run. Finally, find out what type of resources you will have to work with. For instance, if you are being hired to do business development, is the firm willing to spend money on advertising and promotions, or will you just be handed a phone book to do cold calling.

Choosing whether a large or smaller company is best suited for you depends most on your own personality. If you're someone who likes to first understand a process thoroughly before doing it, then a larger company is probably the more suitable environment for you to be in. A larger company gives you more time and room to develop, and offers greater resources and formal training opportunities. However, if you are someone who is mature, aggressive, independent, and enjoys learning-by-doing, then a smaller company environment can be better for you. It is also a good fit for those who like getting involved in many areas and being exposed to a wide variety of challenges, as you can get to see just about everything that goes on in a company.

One of our managers feels that the ideal development environment for a young professional is the representative office of a large international company operating in China. She worked in just such an operation earlier in her career. The rep office had about 20 people. Not only did it offer the professionalism and exposure that she wanted (i.e. it was not a family-style or SOE-type environment), there was also access to the support and resources of the company's overseas headquarters.

Whether within an entrepreneurial start-up or large corporation, it's really a matter of which environment best matches your own personality, manner of doing and learning things, and stage of personal development.

Whether within an entrepreneurial start-up or large corporation, a job opportunity is ultimately what you make of it. Either career paths are proven to be successful ones to follow. It's really a matter of which environment best matches your own personality, manner of doing and learning things, and stage of personal development. Just be sure that the one you choose allows you to develop the skills and experiences you need to further your professional growth.

8) How Do I Get Management To Accept My Ideas?

When trying to get the attention of management, it's important to present your ideas in a professional manner. Many people have terrific ideas and are very willing to share them. For busy managers on the receiving end of such input, however, what they really want to see from their staff is well-packaged ideas that are easily demonstrated and executed.

Rather than just passing ideas to your superiors, put them down in the form of a written proposal. Within the proposal, outline things such as the cost of implementation, time frame to implement, risk factors involved, and most importantly, the bottom-line benefits to the company. Provide analysis and, if possible, proof of the advantages of your idea that is hard to refute. Such a proposal not only reflects the thoroughness that you've put into thinking about a particular problem, but the effort grabs greater attention and consideration from those reviewing your work. If your presentation is sound, then your idea will be difficult to ignore. And by laying out a clear proposal, you will save your management a lot of time and effort in analyzing the implications and benefits of your idea.

In addition, rather than going straight to the top, you might want to first present your idea to someone in the company who can help support and present your proposal to senior management. It might be someone who knows you and your capabilities well, and who has the attention of other senior managers. Such a person is likely to weigh your suggestions more intently and can help develop your idea into an implementable proposal. Ultimately, they can help ensure that your proposal will have an audience.

Throwing out ideas is easy to do. In fact, it can be too easy. Unless presented well, they provide little benefit to busy managers in multinational companies, no matter how good the ideas may be. It's important to be concise and impactful in presenting suggestions to them. Remember, the goal is not to create more work for your manager, but to make their job easier.

9) How Does Someone With A Technical Background Improve Their Career Opportunities?

Unfortunately, the perception of many technical professionals is that their people skills and understanding of business are weak. This is because most of what they do each day usually does not require them to interact with others.

If you value interaction with others as part of your job, start by letting your management know that you wish to have greater involvement with other functional groups, so that you can develop your people skills and exposure to business situations. For instance, you could seek out opportunities to work more closely with the sales team to help them understand the technology or support their pre-sales or post-sales efforts.

A good employer will take an active interest in the long-term career interests of its employees. To help make such interests known, however, you should take the initiative to communicate to your employer your thoughts and ambitions. Try to approach your management for their help and support in giving you greater exposure to other areas. One of the most powerful combinations is a person who has a sound technical background, as well as strong communications skills and business sense. In today's world, where technology and business are so intertwined, such professionals have exceptional value to a wide range of employers.

10) How Do I Explain The Time I Took Off To Prepare For The GRE's And My Future Desire To Study Abroad To An Employer?

In a job interview, I don't believe you need to hide the fact or make up a story about your decision to study for the GRE after university. Applying to graduate school abroad is a natural and reasonable option for many smart, young mainlanders.

Simply tell a prospective employer what is true. That is, you had an idea to study abroad. But after further considering your personal and professional goals, you have decided to gain some work experience instead. Emphasize that what you're most interested in now is a company and job opportunity where you can develop yourself as a professional. As long as your interest and desire are sincere, I don't believe a potential employer can ask anything more of you.

By being honest and up front, you can quickly move past the topic of the time you took off. An employer worth working for should not care about past decisions you've made, beyond what a reasonable explanation can account for. If they do, then you have to question how open-minded they are and if they would be an attractive boss or company to work for anyway. I would even argue that if you scored well on your GRE examination, that this might even indicate to a prospective employer that you are a highly intelligent and motivated person.

11) Do I Have To Repay My Company Back For A Training Course, Should I Leave Earlier Than Expected?

I do not believe there is a legal obligation to repay your company for a training course that they have asked you to take, should you decide to leave soon after completing the course. Unless, that is, you have signed a document stating you are obligated to do so should you leave the company within a certain period of time.

The more important question to ask is, what kind of relationship do you wish to have with your company after you leave. By that, I mean that your relationship with the company may not be a very good one afterwards, if your sudden announcement to leave comes as a big surprise to your management. Understandably, the company would feel a great deal of disappointment in losing you after just having invested so much time and money in your career development.

Should you be asked to repay the training course fee upon your notice to depart, even without a document stating such, you have to evaluate how much you value your continued good standing and relationships within the company you are leaving.

In many situations, your own personal credibility and goodwill may be worth much more than any particular amount of money.

12) How Long Is The Window Of Opportunity?

Many believe that the most exciting time of growth in China will happen over the next ten years, offering an extremely opportune time for mainland professionals to excel. There is a clear shortage of high caliber, bilingual managers in the marketplace. At the same time, however, multinationals are becoming increasingly selective in their hiring. Competition is also increasing all the time, as more local Chinese are gaining experience in international firms or are going abroad to attain university degrees, MBAs, and overseas exposure. Multinationals such as Procter & Gamble and Pepsi even have training "universities" in China to develop local staff more quickly.

The key to staying competitive in the job market is to continually build on new skill sets, according to Joe Wong, the former human resources manager for Northern Telecom in Beijing. "It's all about being able to do things that others can't do," *"The key to staying competitive in the* says Joe. As an example, he points to *job market is to continually build on* the need for good implementers and trainers in China who can pass on *new skill sets. It's all about being able* functional skills and industry expertise *to do things that others can't do."* to local staff.

Although James Yao feels the future outlook for Chinese professionals in multinational firms is very positive, he also warns those about being complacent. "You have to know your value-added out here, then constantly improve on it. When I got to Beijing in 1990, I was a breath of fresh air to customers. Besides just technical skills, I also brought sales and marketing skills that the local information technology industry did not have back then. I even remember organizing one of China's first multimedia presentation, using a barcode projector to show MAC images onto a screen. Today, many others have similar strong technical and sales and marketing backgrounds. But since then, I've acquired general management and strategic market development experience. My ability to stay ahead of the pack is a result of the new expertise and skills I continually work on gaining."

For the time being, the quality and quantity of Mainland Chinese managers needed to satisfy the market demand will not appear overnight. The reality of their widespread presence within multinational senior management ranks is still years away from happening. At the end of the day, by always advancing your know-how and the level of performance you can deliver, you needn't worry so much about changing job market factors.

Chapter 13   Common Mistakes, ... Or, Why Some Don't Make It

So things are looking pretty good. You've just managed to land an excellent position with a leading multinational company. You're excited and motivated about your future prospects. The opportunity is there before you. Yet, it can still all go dramatically wrong. The following are situations you should try to avoid during the course of developing your career in a multinational firm.

Getting Used As Cannon Fodder

Cannon fodder is the term for pieces of shrapnel packed into a cannon. The shrapnel is fired in the general direction of a target, with a hope that it will strike something. It's also a metaphor for eager, young professionals recruited by companies to help them break into the China market. The application of the term comes from a young mainland Chinese working in Shanghai.

I met this person a few years ago. At the time, he was a young graduate who was both confident and highly optimistic about his career prospects. Coming out of university, he was fully prepared to pay his dues. The plastics manufacturing company who hired him had a similar line of thinking, with more than enough tasks to let him prove himself. After a few brief weeks, they sent him to Shenzhen, where he was told to "analyze and improve factory production."

Once at the plant site in Shenzhen, however, the young man was hopelessly over his head. To begin with, the company lacked the management support and a commitment of resources for this objective. He knew next to nothing about factory operations and had no one to guide him. Most disconcerting, he had no idea what his role was. From the time he arrived, he had to carve out for himself both his responsibilities and understanding of how to do things. His frustration and confusion were felt each day.

After persevering in this position for one year, he then came across a large U.S. property development company just getting started in China. Like most multinationals with big plans for the mainland market, this company was salivating over the huge potential. They also happened to be looking for someone bright, hardworking, and willing, who was familiar with China and who spoke good English. Again, the young professional fit the bill. Flattered by the confidence the company managers placed in him, he seized their offer to be their business development manager.

Again, however, he was given minimal training, little supervision, and the vaguest of instructions. It became quickly apparent to him that the company had no well thought out business plan in place to develop the market in China. Although he was not opposed to working hard and knocking on doors, he rarely knew if he was doing the right thing or on the right track. Cannon fodder was what he felt like.

"My company kept pointing and 'firing' me at potential clients hoping I would produce some results," he says. "Each time, I'd end up crashing to the ground. So they'd just load me up and fire me off again to see what kind of information or opportunity I might hit upon."

From the young professional's point of view, he was an expendable body. "With each cannon fodder job I landed myself in, I saw my career prospects dimming," he recalls. "Those were self-defeating situations that only utilized my survival skills, but never provided me with solid professional ones to perform successfully. I knew I needed some real business training and functional expertise if I were to succeed in the long run."

From his experience, he shares this advice for other young professionals. "After two cannon fodder situations, I finally learned how to screen them out. Before, I was easily impressed by job titles and the excitement of working in a multinational company. Back then, every opportunity seemed like a once-in-a-lifetime one to me. Now, however, I insist on clearly defined job responsibilities and company objectives. I ask about what kind of planning that has been done and what kind of support I'll receive. Management must show commitment to the role they want me to play. Without it, you'll be set up for failure. I also take a more realistic account of my own abilities, and an assessment of whether I can attain the objectives expected of me. I know I won't likely have the luxury of a very long ramp up period."

Currently, he is part of a team setting up the China operation of a major U.S. insurance company. He's confident this job presents real potential, as opposed to hyped possibilities. As an indication of the improved outlook of his situation, the first thing the company did when he joined was to send him to Hong Kong for six weeks of training.

Fresh graduates are most susceptible to cannon fodder recruitment and can get caught in such no-win situations. Early in your career, a good training and development environment is the most important thing to consider in your first job. If you're young and inexperienced, but are already considered the expert or most capable person in a particular area for your company, then you really have to wonder how good your company's future prospects are, and ultimately, your own. The young professional was fortunate to be able to jump off the cannon fodder track and onto a real career track. Not everyone is as lucky. The key is to recognize these seemingly attractive, but dead-end jobs, and then avoid them.

Fear Of Failing

For many mainland professionals, their greatest barrier to developing and improving themselves is a fear of failing. Without placing themselves in new, unknown situations, they are unable to gain new skills and pick up new experiences that they need. In the end, it limits their ability to grow and realize greater opportunities in their career.

Jim Leininger works for a well-known training company in Beijing. The programs are primarily targeted for mainland corporate professionals, and emphasize exercises that have little to do with business situations or corporate environments. Instead the activities include anything from physical challenges such as rope climbing or wall scaling, to trying to create a square using a rope with your colleagues, . . . while blind-folded!

"The purpose is to get people to try new things and to create a positive outlook in their approach to life," explains Jim. "We want them to experience new situations and not be afraid to fail. This is bound to happen at times in our career, where problems are encountered that we feel are beyond our capabilities to handle, or where the results of our efforts may fall short of the original objectives that have been set. Every challenge you face though, is a chance to learn something new, about either yourself or a situation. The main point of our exercises is to show that you never lose by trying. That's the attitude and perspective that multinational clients hope their mainland staff will gain when they sign them up for training with us."

Personal Travelogue

Putting Fear Aside

During my Wang Laboratories days, I was sent out as the marketing specialist to support the sales staff in the Taipei office. And that's what I fully intended to do. I wasn't deterred by my poor Mandarin to stop me from performing my job before local customers. I told myself I needed to be committed, persistent, and thick-skinned. So with my 1500-word vocabulary, I constructed and practiced a 90-minute technical marketing presentation about Wang's product lines, corporate strategy, and customer service excellence.

For my first presentation, I was sent down to Kaohsiung in southern Taiwan to speak before a room full of nearly 100 very technical and local information technology managers. Most were from government offices or large Taiwan companies. Many attended my seminar in their company work uniforms.

I recalled how I used to always see non-native, English-speaking Asians give presentations in their halted English. Their delivery was reserved and uncomfortable. That wasn't going to be the case for me. After all, I was professionally trained as an MBA in presentation skills. I proceeded to deliver my Mandarin presentation in an animated and confident manner. I used eye-contact, voice intonation, and body language to effectively communicate my point. I paced the floor with energy and conviction, preaching the glories of Wang computers.

In my mind, I was speaking fluent Mandarin. I sounded smooth and coherent, the way I would sound in English. "At Wang Computers, we have the best technology that can fit your business needs." But with a limited vocabulary and a few textbook sentence structures at my disposal, what they were actually hearing was more like: "No matter your company's needs, Wang. have good computers."

And because of my inability to express certain points as creatively as I would in English, some phrases I would repeat up to a dozen times. I can only imagine what that was like to hear. "Yes, Wang computers are very good and very cheap ... very cheap and good ... extremely good, and not a lot of money."

One thing I have to say though, I never saw anyone in the audience not paying attention. Their eyes were glued to me. I believe they were just completely stunned at what they were seeing before them. A dichotomy of a seemingly competent, intelligent adult man giving a high-level business presentation, only speaking like an eight year old child. And doing it with such fervor and enthusiasm.

In the end, however, they were very receptive. I believe they sensed my sincere desire to communicate with them on their terms. And I believe that my intelligence and willingness to work with them came through. Ultimately, I was able to make a memorable impression that helped me establish relationships with these customers.

Job Hopping

Recently, I was reviewing the resume of a candidate applying for a finance position in Shanghai. He was 28 years old and seeking his fourth job in five years. His resume looked horrible. But changing jobs frequently is not uncommon for capable professionals in China, where they find it easy to attract opportunities. For those with good educational backgrounds and some initial work experience, there's always another position out there that pays higher. And there are always other jobs that sound more exciting and glamorous given the amount of growth that multinationals are experiencing. The result of such movement, however, can be extremely damaging to your career in the long run. For this candidate, he had quickly reached a point where his stability, commitment, and career objectives were all in question.

Sam Su is the CEO for Greater China of Tricon Restaurants International. He is the head of the region and country manager for China. At the time he took charge of China operations, there were four Kentucky Fried Chicken restaurants (a.k.a. KFC) in China. Now, he oversees over 400 locations. Sam's advice to young mainland professionals on developing one's career is straightforward. "Focus on building solid business skills and on acquiring know-how. Be well-rounded and constantly expand your comfort zone of abilities. I see a lot of mainlanders go from one position to the next for incremental salary increases every year or two. It's short-sighted. You should

"You should think about what the resume of a CEO looks like. They get to where they are by showing they can build a business and get substantial results."

think about what the resume of a CEO looks like. They get to where they are by showing they can build a business and get substantial results. That takes at least three to five years to do in most situations. You shouldn't make career decisions based on what you can get now. You need to remember that your career is 30 or 40 years long. What does a few thousand RMB mean now compared to what you could make one day as a senior executive for a major company? More important is to consider how much you can grow in each opportunity and to always show performance and prove yourself before moving on."

Staying with one organization for more than just a year or two also improves your ability to get results in the company you're with, particularly in large multinationals with several China and international operations. Not only does your knowledge of how to get things done in the organization grow over time, but others in the company become more familiar with you and your abilities as well. Cecelia Xi has worked with Ford Motors since 1995. "So much has happened in the past six years," says Cecelia. "Seeing the history and growth of the company's operation in China lets me understand the changes, dynamics, and personalities in the organization. That's a valuable benefit in helping me do my job well."

How Many Job Changes Are Too Many?

When I see a resume that averages a new job every 12-24 months, that's quite a lot of different companies and positions. That means that by the time you are 30 years old, you'll have worked for four or five companies. That's too many. Two or perhaps three positions at that age is much more reflective of someone who is stable and who takes a mature approach towards their career.

"I'm wary of golden eagles and high flyers, whose mentality is to learn what they can and then move on," says Frank Chen. "They're results driven, but think that job hopping is the way to get ahead. What they don't realize is that after ten years, their resume looks like a smorgesborg. I tell all my staff that they need to pay their dues. When I review a resume, I look for stability above all else. I want to see at least one job that has lasted at least three or four years, not one to two in each case. I won't even consider those. Many mainland professionals need to understand that, eventually, it's a detriment to their career."

The Sun Won't Always Be Shining

When the economic picture is bright, changing jobs can appear to be a fast, easy way to escalate both your job title and salary. and seem like a shrewd approach to developing your career. But you shouldn't count on such unending prosperity. Over the past six to eight years, the rapid development of markets and the expansion of multinational firms in the mainland has created a period of greater demand than supply for qualified managers and professional staff.

However, although China's long-term economic signs are positive, inevitably there are downturn periods where companies are forced to look more closely at the compensation levels of each staff relative to the value they provide. It's during such times that the situation for job hoppers becomes the most uncertain. Their inflated salaries stand out as overpriced against the questionable experience they provide. Their marketability becomes tenuous. That's when patience and perseverance emerge as the most desirable virtues to have in developing your career.

When Is It Okay To Switch Jobs Early?

We don't normally recommend to people that they switch jobs less than a year in a particular position. However, there are times when we'll meet a young professional with a good attitude and strong desire to do a good job. But it is apparent that continuing in their current situation is harming their career development and personal motivation. Perhaps they are being asked to perform a task where it is highly unlikely that they'll succeed. Or they have selected a job or industry that is clearly not suited for them. For instance, their job requires them to do sales, but once they've started they realize that they would perform much better in an operations role. The most compelling reason to leave a job early, however, is that their boss or company do not appear to take any type of interest in their career development or success.

Of course, the best way to avoid situations where you need to depart shortly after joining is to be more thorough in choosing a job in the first place. In looking for your next position, focus on better understanding the nature of both the industry and company you'll be joining, as well as the type of daily situations and people you'll be dealing with. There are many positions, companies, and situations out there where dedication and effort are appreciated and nurtured, and that can be very satisfying to you. Finding the right one is a matter of knowing what you want and understanding what you're getting into.

Too Eager/Too Demanding

Jeffrey Reed sees the mainlanders employed in multinational companies as among the best and brightest within a nation of 1.3 billion people. He finds the ones that he's worked with to have a terrific sense of hard work, better even than most professionals he's worked with abroad. However, the exceptional caliber of these mainland professionals presents a double-edged sword. As great as their potential is, their expectations can be just as unrealistic.

Perhaps the biggest challenge today for multinational companies is managing the expectations of their mainland staff, who tend to be too anxious to move ahead. "As soon as many of them see some initial success, they think they are ready to run the company," says Jeffrey. "When you tell them that you don't believe they're ready yet, they get frustrated and upset. They become difficult to manage because they aren't satisfied with the responsibilities and opportunities they are receiving. They spend too much time and energy thinking about getting promoted to their next position, rather than about getting results within their current one."

Many mainland professionals expect to move up the organization based on their seniority and credentials. When they see someone else get promoted around them, they feel that they are entitled to a promotion as well. Where career advancement in a Chinese enterprise is often related to tenure, it is based on performance and achievement in a multinational organization. Within multinationals, it is not merely an evolutionary process. It is earned.

Cecelia Xi: It's Only A Title

Personal History: *33 years old. Born and raised in Shanghai*
Parents: *One teaches primary school and one teaches middle school*
Education: *B.A. in English from Shanghai International Studies University*

Cecelia on holiday in Europe

The first time I met Cecelia Xi was over lunch in Beijing. What impressed me during our meeting was how expressive and confident she came across in a two-hour conversation that took place entirely in English. Her professionalism, as well as energy and enthusiasm were apparent. She mentioned how excited she was about her upcoming trip to Hong Kong and Singapore. It was to be her first time traveling abroad!

Cecelia joined Ford Motor Company in February of 1995. It is the first and only multinational company she has worked for. Beginning as an executive assistant to the director of the import/export department, she often functioned as an interpreter in management meetings. The position exposed her to a variety of business situations and gave her a chance to interface with expatriate managers. When the operation moved from Shanghai to Beijing, she was transferred to the human resources department as a training coordinator and became a certified trainer in ten corporate development courses. The position allowed her to work closely with four training managers, each from a diverse background. From them, she learned how to bridge Chinese and western cultural differences. Today, Cecelia reports to Ford's China human resources director.

Being involved in high profile projects has been a consistent theme throughout her career with Ford. "I believe it's because management knows that I'm willing to get involved," says Cecelia. "I'll always go out of my way to assist others, even to the point of initiating tasks or volunteering when a situation arises."

Cecelia also maintains one basic approach to her job. "When asked for help, I never say, "no, I can't do it," she says. She identifies her father, who is a teacher, as the person who has most influenced her ability to tackle problems and look for creative solutions. "I'll always think about a problem that is presented, and try to respond later with at least one idea. I also try not to stop at just understanding things at a superficial level. I want to understand the purpose of what I am doing. Therefore, I'll try to ask questions that go deeper into the issue."

After hearing about the high-level projects she has worked on, I asked Cecelia if she thought she could get a director title in another company. "I know I could jump to another opportunity that might offer me that," responded Cecelia. "But there is so much title inflation in China. What I care about is job content, in terms of the complexity of work, impact on the company, and upward mobility of a position. My current position gives me all those opportunities and more."

"Whenever I'm facing a career decision, I look at my bottom-line and work out the worst case scenario," she continues. "For me, it's, can I survive the loss? Or, is the gain worth more than the risk? For instance, in 1998, I took a six-month assignment with Ford's JMC joint venture factory in Nanchang. Compared to Beijing or Shanghai, it's probably not a location that is on the top of most people's lists. Although it is considered a third tier city, the experience I gained from going there was invaluable. I made the move because I could see the benefit to me. As a technical training coordinator, I was asked to be involved in a product development department restructuring. The work I did on that project is still something I'm most proud of today."

Cecelia's current role as the employee development and recruitment manager gives her responsibility for expatriate placements in China, where she works closely with home countries and overseas offices. The assignment allows her to develop her business planning skills and strategic sense, and gain greater exposure to the company's overall business. "For my career, I don't want to be seen as just a local Chinese employee," says Cecelia. "I want to develop myself in ways where I'll be valued as a global employee." If you were to ever meet her, there would be no doubt in your mind that she is well on her way to being just that.

Moving Up Too Fast

One 25 years old had been working for three years as a production assistant manager for an international computer components manufacturer in Suzhou. He was doing well in his company, and was told by his boss that he had excellent potential to be a manager. He was promised this opportunity in the near future. Unfortunately, this only made him feel frustrated, to the point that he contemplated leaving the company.

My advice to him was to spend a little more time in his current position before taking on such a big jump in responsibility. Twenty-five years old is still so early in a person's career. He should be taking this time to build the depth of his knowledge and experience. Although I'm sure he's learned a lot about production in three years, there are certainly many more things he could understand better. In his case, it would probably be better for him in the long-run to give himself a little more time to develop further.

As an example, when I began my career as a design engineer for a toy company in the U.S., I was promoted three times within my first five years. However, I was still another two to three years away from reaching a manager level in the company. This is the norm in more mature job markets such as the U.S. These days in China, however, the tendency for many multinationals is to promote very quickly. The pressure to do so is high, given the fast growth and competitive nature of many industries here. The result is seemingly fast, attractive promotion tracks for mainland professionals. Many can end up derailed, however, if they are given greater roles before they are prepared to handle them.

In China now, the plus side is, if you are very good, you can move up quickly. However, the minus side is that many good people are promoted before they are ready and end up getting set back in their careers. When I speak with multinational executives, they typically express that they would prefer not to promote staff as fast as they are doing. In too many cases, mainland professionals have not received enough of the experience that they need to handle the level of responsibility they are being asked to take on. And in too many cases, the lack of proper training and time to prepare themselves adequately results in their failing in their first attempt as managers. As a result, the experience actually ends up being damaging to their career.

Jeffrey Reed had one such instance with a promising mainland manager in his organization. "Two years ago, we promoted one of our top middle managers to run one of our food divisions. In retrospect, his move up in our organization was clearly too fast. The promotion created an unexpected insecurity in the manager. Rather than manage with a true confidence based on expertise and experience, he started to impose himself on his staff by reverting to authority and rule. It was a completely autocratic management style that his staff did not respond to. I don't believe he did this intentionally, but subconsciously it was the only way he felt he could command respect. Instead of being open and communicative like a strong manager should be, he became hard-line and dictatorial. Gradually, he lost the ability to get results out of those around him. In the end, he had to leave the company because his failure left him without a future in our organization. It was a real shame and waste of an excellent employee."

Managing people well is a challenging, ongoing learning process. Jumping into that responsibility too soon can result in failure and do real harm to a person's professional development. Be sure your readiness to manage is based on genuine capabilities and knowledge. That way, you'll more likely be able to lead in a secure and successful manner.

Career Suicide

A year ago, I met a bright, confident woman in her early 20s in Beijing. At the time, she had just joined a well-known international public relations agency. It was a good opportunity and environment for her to learn the fundamentals of this industry. After six months, however, I heard she changed jobs and had begun working for a small, local pr firm. Apparently, she wanted to be promoted to a higher title, which the international firm did not feel she was ready for yet. Being less established and anxious to bring on board someone with international agency experience, the local firm was more than happy to give her a manager title.

Three months later, the young woman called to tell me that she had just joined an Internet start-up as their director of marketing communications. The company was founded by two people she met through friends, who were just a few years older than her. Soon after joining, many newly established Internet businesses in China began to feel the realities of competing in an immature on-line market. Four months later, I heard that the start-up went out of business and that the woman had opened her own company.

Because of her priority and desire to attain higher positions with each company she was with, she had effectively managed to commit career suicide. Within a span of just over one year, she had worked for three companies. Her promotions, rather than being based on merit and performance, were based on short-term, opportunistic situations. Although her titles increased, the quality of her experience and the environment she placed herself into decreased with each move. She was barely 25 years old, but her frequent job moves to less reputable companies made both her resume and herself look undesirable to any company valuing high professional standards. Although she had become a "*lao ban*," her title held little weight or credibility without a track record of prior accomplishments. In essence, she had come down to one of her last remaining options, employing herself.

Success Does Not Come Overnight

Some candidates I meet are entirely unrealistic about the time frame it will take to achieve the professional goals they've set. They expect to make quantum leaps in their career advancement despite their lack of strong language skills, market knowledge, or professional training that are necessary to succeed.

Often, it just takes a while for your break to happen. There are many who have successfully switched into jobs and industries they had little previous background in. Their success did not come immediately though. Instead, they first leveraged the strength of their work experience to find a good position. They were then able to develop their network of contacts and understanding of the new industry they entered.

"The most important thing I did was to figure out where I wanted to be in a few years. After that, I just tried to take realistic steps and show people what I could do whenever I had the chance."

Once over those initial hurdles, you'll find that your job prospects can change dramatically. After you've established yourself as a solid performer who is able to make contributions, both the opportunities and your ability to take advantage of them improves exponentially. As the group account director of a U.S. advertising agency in Beijing put it, "The most important thing I did was to figure out where I wanted to be in a few years. After that, I just tried to take realistic steps and show people what I could do whenever I had the chance."

Of the many success stories I've written about, luck or timing contributed to some extent. However, each one involved hard work and some degree of patience by the individual. In looking at their resume, professional growth and achievements were clear to see. When their opportunities came, they were ready. Although you may have a particular level of achievement in mind, give things time to happen and enjoy the ride along the way.

Poor Interpersonal Skills

Lillian Liu is the Director of Human Resources in China for Compaq Computers in Beijing. Throughout her career, management has identified her as a high potential employee. In 1997, her company at the time, Nortel Networks, sent her to the U.S. to spend six months at corporate headquarters, and another 12 months studying for her MBA in North Carolina.

Lillian began her career in the hospitality industry. At the time, she did not foresee how valuable her years working for a leading international hotel in Shanghai would be to her future success. "While working at Holiday Inn, being friendly and helpful to people became second nature," she says. "Basically, that was my job. Now, I don't think twice about chatting with people when I see them, or making an effort to engage a colleague."

Many Mainland Chinese, however, are not comfortable doing that. They make little attempt to establish a rapport with their co-workers, particularly those from other departments. They exclude themselves from other groups, or may even exclude others from themselves. And when they do deal with others in the company, they do so in a formal manner and only if a problem arises or if they need some help.

"It doesn't work that way, however, in situations where you need to work well with others to get results," says Lillian. "Most Chinese professionals I see are unquestionably capable. Within their own job scope, they know their responsibilities and respond well when called upon. However, when it comes to working with people in other departments or being involved on projects that require the coordination of cross-functional resources, the networks to succeed are just not there. A main reason is that they've made little previous effort to establish any type of relationship with other co-workers."

These people will refer to idle conversation or simple exchanges with others as "nonsense talking." Of course, you could call it that and look at it in that way. However, you could also just call it being sociable. Conversations don't need to be lengthy or meaningful. It's about the ability to communicate and work effectively with others. It doesn't take much beyond trying to share common interests or make an effort to be friendly.

In Lillian's experience as a human resources professional who regularly resolves internal company conflicts as part of her job, working out issues is much easier if you have an existing relationship with the other party. It doesn't have to be a deep one, but friendly goes a long way. Then, people are able to deal with each other as human beings, rather than as subordinates or departmental rivals. Within multinational companies, interpersonal skills are especially important in developing relationships with management who come from other countries. Such skills help facilitate cooperation at high levels where teamwork among cross-cultural parties becomes even more critical.

"My ability to make others feel comfortable helps me get the results I need to deliver in my job," says Lillian. "When I have to resolve issues involving people from other departments, they know me and know they can deal with me. Our management also involves me as a resource in a lot of company issues. They know that I can understand many of the nuances, priorities, and perspectives of both our local staff and foreign managers. Ultimately, they feel that I can be counted on as someone who can be a link between the two sides to handle a lot of situations better."

"I'm not talking about playing politics," Lillian is quick to add. "There is a line between politics and doing the things that will help you gain the best result for both yourself and the company. The reality is that the better you can communicate with others, and vice versa, the more likely you are to succeed in the organization you're a part of."

Personal Travelogue

Don't Underestimate People Skills

During my initial few months in Taipei with Wang Laboratories, I spent several weeks working on a proposal for a major government client. This was one of my first chances to show my value to the local operations, particularly to the sales force and rest of the marketing team. I prepared cost comparisons and business process studies to justify why our computer system was the obvious solution to go with. After finishing, I showed my Taiwanese colleague my impressive report. I marveled at the spreadsheets, workflow diagrams, and bulleted critical points I had put together.

My colleague nodded and smiled in his typical manner as I provided him with a concise summary of each key point in my analysis. Although he always gave me his undivided attention, his enthusiasm and intensity rarely matched my own. Seldom did he have any comments to add to my work. After finishing my presentation, I asked him what he thought. He paused for a second, looking a bit perplexed. There was no response. Suddenly, his face lit up, as if suddenly struck with a revolutionary idea. With complete earnestness, he looked at me and said: "Have you thought about taking them out to lunch?"

I was stunned. "Lunch?!? Why didn't I think of that?" I sarcastically thought to myself. "You've got to be kidding. I am a finely tuned, well-trained MBA! Give me a break."

The next day, I presented to the client my study as planned. Although they appeared to be impressed by my analysis, they did not end up contracting us for the project I proposed.

Today, I'd do it differently. There's a saying in Chinese, "do business with your head, but use your heart." You may have the right professional experience, but without the sensitivity and understanding of the parties you are dealing with, it can mean very little. My colleague was right. I needed to put an effort into building a personal relationship with the client. Particularly, in that situation, where I was an outsider. I needed to let the client understand and know me better, and vice versa. No wonder my colleague used to do so well without performing pre-sales work or feasibility studies. I'm sure back then he must have been thinking to himself: "MBA, SchMBA."

Resolving Cultural Loyalty

Some mainlanders are reluctant, or flat out refuse to speak English. They'll only speak Chinese with other overseas or regional Chinese, claiming as the reason their loyalty to and pride in their Chinese heritage. The limitation holds them back from improving this critical skill needed to succeed in an international business environment, and from establishing relationships with foreign management and overseas colleagues whose knowledge can be important for their professional growth.

However, of the mainland professionals I know who have developed broader international skill-sets and perspectives, many are the proudest I have met in terms of their being Chinese. Gefei Li's pride as a Chinese and his belief in the capabilities of Chinese people run deep. Yet, he also has a tremendous interest in learning more about world-class practices and business approaches from abroad. How does he resolve the two?

Gefei identifies the importance of being in tune with your basic values and comfortable with your own identity. "Being out of touch with them can create a lack of confidence, and cause people to react defensively to new situations," says Gefei. "If you're able to appreciate and feel secure about who you are and where you come from, then you won't be threatened by trying new things that can improve your capabilities, opportunities, and even quality of life."

Being part of a multinational company should not be over-glamorized. This can cause some mainlanders to position themselves at an inferior level, and inhibits them from voicing opinions to foreign managers when necessary. It can also cause some to feel resentful and create a view that working in a multinational is a necessary evil that they must go through to get ahead. They are reluctant to get more involved, for fear of compromising or selling out their Chinese identity. The result is that they hold themselves back from chances for interaction and development that can help them realize greater opportunities. Working in a multinational company does not imply lack of pride in one's culture or heritage. It's merely an environment that offers chances that can bring about personal and professional benefits.

Don't Waste Opportunities

What a multinational environment offers, however, should also not be diminished. Sharon Dong is very straightforward with her staff about this. Sharon is the managing director in Shanghai of Octagon Prism, an international events management company with operations throughout Asia. Previous to Octagon Prism, Sharon worked for four years in both Shanghai and Hong Kong with one of the world's top five public relations agencies. She tells her staff that working for a multinational company offers them an excellent opportunity that they should take full advantage of.

The problem she sees in some of her employees is that once they get into an international company, they feel like they've already made it. As a result, they do not continue to push themselves in the manner that they should. In a recent situation, Sharon hired a young woman from a prestigious university. While walking through the office one afternoon, she happened to notice this person sitting at her desk playing a computer card game. The office had just completed a hectic, but successful product launch for a major client. There was a slowdown in the office's activity, until the next big project deadline. When Sharon asked this person if she had enough work to do, the staff casually looked at her to tell her that she was bored.

Sharon thought that answer to be incredible to hear. Immediately, she asked the young woman to give her five names from their client list. The woman's eyes went wide, and there was a deathly silence. "You're in a new company and part of an industry that is new to you," Sharon continued. "There are so many things that you need to learn to do this job well. If you're sitting around and feeling bored, it's not my fault. It means that you're a bad employee. I've told you how to access our client files and encouraged you to read up on their company backgrounds. It is not my, nor anyone else's job to hold your hand. Try taking some initiative." The point was made, and she never saw this woman idle at her desk again.

Actually, Sharon can understand the feeling among her young staff. They are smart, well educated, and highly sought. They feel that they know a lot, when they haven't really proven anything yet. They often feel that they should be given more challenging things to do, and sit around waiting for opportunities to be handed to them. Sharon also felt that way when she first started out. That's changed as she has matured over the years.

"Because my English was very good when I was younger, I used to hear compliments from others all the time. As a result, I thought I was something special. It's funny, but the older I get, the less I seem to know," says Sharon with a laugh. "Of course, my business knowledge and expertise are much greater now than when I began my career. But the more I'm exposed to situations and have the chance to interact with excellent people, the more I realize how much there is that I still need to learn."

"The positive effect is that I'm much more appreciative today of the situations I'm in. I see more and learn quicker. Most importantly, I have genuine confidence now, rather than an arrogance of being good. It's because I know I'm actually very competent at what I do, and not because I think I'm good or because others say I am. When you're dealing with mature professionals, their caliber and excellence come out the minute they open their mouth. It should never have to be the case where you have to tell others that they exist."

Ask And You Shall Receive

When it comes to gaining greater responsibility and exposure, many mainland professionals take the approach that "if my boss is any good, he'll recognize my good work and contribution." Or, they believe that "if he valued me, he would notice and give me more opportunities." However, it might be the case where your manager is just too busy. Or, it could be that what you perceive to be his viewpoint might not be the way he thinks at all. Such assumptions can result in a lot of time wasted and opportunities missed.

In managing your career, it is important that you go and ask for what you need. You'll often be surprised at management's response. I'm not referring to requests for promotions and higher job titles, but rather, seeking additional job responsibilities and chances for greater involvement. Most international companies and managers I'm aware of are willing to support that type of desire in their employees.

For young professionals especially, once you've gotten into a good situation, be proactive. Do anything you can to show what you can do. If there's something that you're interested in, ask if you can get involved in some way. If you're capable, the opportunity can happen very quickly. For instance, I've promoted three of my company's office administration staff into consultant positions within their first six months in our company. It's because their potential was plain to see. Their work ethic, resourcefulness, and quality of work were clearly demonstrated each day and in every task that they were required to handle in their job scope, and then some.

Chapter 14　Glass Ceiling?

Over the past year, I have raised the topic of the glass ceiling in multinationals in China with many of those I've interviewed for this book. Opinions varied dramatically, depending on whether the person had an employee or management perspective. It also depended greatly on the multinational company they worked for.

The future for multinational firms in China is clear. The bottom line is, they cannot operate profitably using expats throughout their management ranks. As a result, Susan Pattis believes that, for the most part, the glass ceiling is an illusion for many mainland professionals. From a business perspective, multinationals are committed to identifying and developing their Chinese staff. While many mainland professionals complain about a glass ceiling barrier, they fail to recognize that they might not yet be ready to command the management and revenue responsibilities of a multinational business operating in China.

Real Or Perceived?

Whether a glass ceiling exists or not depends on each company's philosophy. Some multinationals want their home office expats to continue to represent their corporate interests in China. Reasons are rooted in the level of comfort that a company's headquarters would like to feel, with regard to trust and control. They prefer having their own home-grown executives in place looking after critical aspects of the business. Others want to localize their China operation, but their decision to promote Chinese managers is overwhelmingly driven by cost reasons. Such companies usually lack a management and resource commitment, and never seem to get it right in setting up and executing their localization plans. Within these organizations, employees often complain of facing a glass ceiling that restricts their advancement opportunities.

Some multinationals, however, are fully committed to placing their mainland operation in the hands of Chinese managers. Their willingness to localize their management team is rooted in a fundamental belief that this is the right, long-term approach to operating their business in China. For these companies, you don't see or sense indications of a glass ceiling. The commitment is demonstrated in the company's efforts to help their mainland staff gain the exposure and develop relationships they need to enter into and succeed in management ranks. Among the client companies that she works with, Susan sees more and more foreign managers treating their mainland staff as partners, and not just as policeman to execute and reinforce the organization's policies and business plan.

Almost Too Aggressive

From his own experience, Frank Chen does not see a glass ceiling. His past two multinational companies aggressively localized their management staff in the mainland, perhaps too quickly even. For instance, his current employer recently went from over 100 to 25 expats in one year. "Our Chinese managers have been told that by 2003, the only position that will be an expat one will be the general manager's," says Frank. "They know they have to step up and start making some of the big decisions. There's no more Mr. Expat Boss to ask the question, "What do we do?" Now, they are the Expat Boss!"

Frank can sense the insecurity among many of his company's mainland managers who will soon be assuming these key leadership roles. In his opinion, the rapid transition is putting many into front-line management positions before they are ready. "They're only in their early thirties and usually carry more responsibility than what they've been trained to handle at that point," continues Frank. "Compared to the career advancement pace for professionals in the West, mainland professionals here are getting promoted much too soon in many cases."

"Compared to the career advancement pace for professionals in the West, mainland professionals here are getting promoted much too soon in many cases."

Christina Fang also does not believe in the glass ceiling based on what she sees in her company. "Our senior management would love to promote our mainland staff into higher level positions," she says. "But they can't identify enough ones who they feel are ready yet. Taking on management responsibilities in a multinational company requires more from a person than just demonstrating competencies and performance. Mainland staff need to build their understanding of other aspects of the business and gain cross functional experience. Relationships with overseas parties also need to be developed. As future managers, they must be able to talk the language of business with fluency and depth with both senior management and home office."

Unfortunately, the lack of commitment to promote mainland staff into management roles still persists among many multinational firms and senior managers. Christina knows expat managers who have been working in China for five years, but who still have nobody beneath them within three years of being a qualified replacement for their position. For these expats, they are in no hurry to vacate their positions. Or, their mentality is, "I'm out of here in a few years, why should I help them." Or, rather than develop or hire the best talent to be groomed, they might hire or promote the second best to give themselves more time to remain in China.

Mainlanders at senior management levels are widespread today within finance and sales functions. However, their absence still exists in many other functional areas. For instance, there aren't many mainland marketing professionals with ten years of experience, or public relations professionals with more than six years of experience. That situation is changing rapidly though. Within the next five years, Christina believes that even the overseas background that she offers will be replaced by a locally-trained mainland Chinese. "One of my main objectives is to establish a Mainland Chinese management team in our company," says Christina. "The future is really theirs."

More Local Companies Are Offering Excellent Opportunities

Despite the career development that multinationals offer, local companies are starting to draw the interest of those who have usually sought positions within multinational firms only. Private Chinese companies are beginning to compete with leading international ones by developing the same high caliber management expertise and business practices. To do this, they must employ the same talent and skill sets of similar quality as those nurtured in multinational companies. In a Chinese firm, professionals with international caliber capabilities can command greater responsibilities and handle opportunities beyond what other local staff may be given.

Amy Chu began her career working six years for a U.S. public relations firm in Shanghai. Recently, she found a position as an account director for a local public relations firm. She reports directly to the executive director and supervises a staff of six account managers and executives. "Our management values the different ideas and viewpoints I have on operation issues and how we conduct our business," says Amy. She feels she is better able to address issues that many of her colleagues back off from. Amy also serves an unofficial role as the right-hand person to the executive director. Recently, she has been asked to build up and head the company's marketing department.

Local companies attempting to do business overseas are also offering excellent opportunities to well-trained professionals, where management may put you at the forefront of their international business activities. The result is a chance to stand out and have an impact on the company's overseas business success. Sandra Wang worked for several years with a European consumer products manufacturer in Shenzhen. She now works for a local mainland toy manufacturer that provides baby toys for U.S. companies such as Gund and Kids II. "Our company is continually venturing into new deals with other U.S. customers," says Sandra. "Because I can comfortably deal within an international environment, I'm part of the company's efforts to develop business with western clients."

This past year, Sandra has traveled to the U.S. three times with top management to solicit business from new clients. Her role during the trips is to communicate in meetings her company's capabilities and resources in China.

It's not only your company that may value you, but the foreign clients you work with as well. Sandra notices the sense of security and clarity of communication she provides to her company's U.S. clients. "They feel confident knowing they're dealing with someone who can understand their expectations and is familiar with their way of thinking. When an important issue needs to be resolved, they'll often ask to speak with me to make sure their point gets across accurately."

The drawback for Sandra and Amy is working in corporate structures and business styles that often involve nuances in office politics, decision making, and situations that are not normally encountered to the same degree in multinational company settings. "Whereas you can more freely and directly express your opinions in an international company, in a Chinese enterprise you often have to find a way to communicate your point without offending others or coming across as a know-it-all," says Amy. "That makes it most important to have a boss who will support you and who really understands your capabilities."

Overall, they both feel that at this point in their careers, working in a Chinese company gives them a faster, stronger career development track than if they remained in a multinational. They are acquiring overseas business experience, dealing with international customers, and receiving greater management responsibilities overall, beyond what they could attain in their previous companies. Given the improving standards, increasing internationalization, and more aggressive business objectives of Chinese enterprises, they believe they are in a promising situation that will result in excellent long-term success.

Part VI

The Wrap Up

Chapter 15 Future Prospects In China: New Companies And New Opportunities

Our World-Class Mainland Company

The New Generation Of Mainland Companies

Even up to a couple of years ago, just about the only opportunities that existed for mainlanders to gain exposure to international caliber experience and business practices was to work for a multinational company. The management expertise and professionalism of international firms were far above what Chinese companies could offer. Today, however, a growing number of Chinese-founded and run enterprises are matching the professional standards of their multinational counterparts.

Among Internet businesses in China, names such as Eachnet and 51job.com are among the best regarded. In addition to being in an excellent position to be the top players in their category, they all have one other thing in common. They all happen to be led by mainland Chinese nationals. Most are returnees who have studied and worked abroad for a few years. Rather than SOE work backgrounds, they have received their professional training from top international graduate programs and world-class companies. However, they are also distinctly mainland Chinese in their roots and orientation.

Shao Yi Bo is a good example of such a returnee. He left China at age 17 to attend Harvard University. After four years, he graduated with degrees in Engineering, Physics, and Economics. As a highly sought graduate, he was employed by the Boston Consulting Group, one of the world's top consulting firms. Two years later, BCG sponsored Bo's return to Harvard, this time to attain his MBA.

Upon his graduation in May of 1999, China's Internet industry was in its newborn state. The temptation was too great. With an idea in mind to start one of the mainland's first auction sites and the ground floor timing of the industry in China, Bo resigned from BCG and co-founded his Internet company, Eachnet. The move involved high personal risk and was a bold roll of the dice by Bo.

Today, Eachnet is the leading Internet auction site in China. With over 130 employees and several major investment institutions backing the business, the outlook for the company is promising.

Same Practices, Same Quality

Companies like Eachnet represent a new generation of businesses that are mainland Chinese in origin, and that are utilizing world-class standards and business practices to establish themselves as industry leaders. Similar to Bo, his senior management team have gained their work experience from leading international companies like Proctor & Gamble, McKinsey & Company, and others. With them, they bring to and provide Eachnet with the same knowledge of business concepts, management styles, and expertise used by the world's most successful companies.

As a result, mainland companies such as Eachnet are beginning to offer similar career development benefits that were previously offered by multinationals only. They possess both an insider status to the mainland market, as well as a firm understanding of international business practices. They are identified by investors as being able to perform well in China, and by mainland customers as being able to offer the best products and services on the market. They are providing mainland professionals with the chance to be a part of a business that may become a major player within its industry in China.

Increasingly, these companies are offering the type of environment that allow Chinese professionals to gain the quality exposure and experience they wish to acquire. They have a cultural perspective that are familiar to mainlanders, but also a business and management approach that exhibits itself in a world-class manner.

Bridging The Gap

The first time I realized the tremendous shortage of and opportunities for people capable of effectively facilitating business between China and the rest of the world was during a trip to Los Angeles in 1994. The trip was a personal visit, but I happened to have a meeting with the international vice president and the general manager of a growing telecommunications company based in California. They were looking to market and distribute their products and services in Greater China. However, they had never been to China before and knew little about the mainland's telecommunications infrastructure, state of technology, or presence of other telecom firms. They lacked the answer to even some of the most basic questions regarding how to do business in China. The encounter was an unexpected eye opener.

Three things became apparent to me then. The first was that there was a huge lack of information and knowledge about China among U.S. companies and individuals wanting to do business here. China was still a black hole for most. For U.S. parties, the obstacles for doing mainland business are basic ones. What resources are available? What expertise already exists? And how does one access them?

The second was that the marketing of China abroad, and its resources and capabilities, were practically nonexistent. Despite the growing availability and quality of expertise, services, and information that can be found for doing business in China, they are effectively communicated to those outside the mainland by very few individuals and companies.

For example, if you were a foreigner who wanted to do business in China, who could you think of to contact and work with? Perhaps a major multinational that you'd assume would have China operation. For instance, if you were looking for consulting support to help you understand and enter the China market, well-known firms like McKinsey & Company or The Boston Consulting Group may come to mind.

These firms are unquestionably proven and highly respected worldwide. But what is their actual China expertise? What is their local knowledge in a particular industry? Do they have relationships to channels, as well as access to resources that can open doors to local markets? And beyond their capabilities, can every company wanting to do business in China afford the fees that these international consulting firms charge?

In fact, there are other highly competent resources and consulting services in China that are equally, if not more, knowledgeable about mainland markets and business for just about every industry out there. These are firms whose businesses are rooted and solely focused in China. Their expertise, communications skills, and professional practices are equivalent to those offered by multinationals, since the people in these companies are themselves trained from within multinationals originally. They've moved on to begin their own business or be a part of a smaller, start-up organization.

Identifying these alternative resources is difficult, however, because their existence outside of China is virtually unknown. The consulting industry example can be easily repeated for many other services and industries. For instance, who would you seek out for regional public relations and media expertise, market entry and business development support, or distribution and partnering resources? It's a common problem faced by foreign parties wanting to do business in China.   .

The last realization I had was that beyond market knowledge and the expertise to help them navigate the mainland's business environment, these two international managers were eager to work with someone who spoke their language, could key into their issues, and understood their thinking. These qualities were critical in gaining their confidence and trust in dealing with someone who could help them do business in China.

Occupying the Middle Ground

There is an unlimited array of products, services, and technologies from abroad that companies would like to introduce to China, during a period of development where the country is aggressively seeking to raise its overall standard of living and quality of life. The needs and interests are there. The key challenge is the difficulty that business parties from both sides have in attracting and cooperating with each other. And a main limiting factor to closer, more effective transaction is the critical resource of individuals and services that can deliver China business expertise and market access to international parties.

Not every company or individual seeking to do business in China is a Fortune 1000 company in size. There are many successful international firms with annual revenues in the tens to hundreds of million US dollars, that seek local expertise and services to help them build their business in China. These firms are open to working with more affordable, alternative resources, rather than what large multinationals offer.

There is a critical middle ground that needs to be bridged in many areas. Businesses and individuals from both sides are all trying to better understand

There is a critical middle ground that needs to be bridged in many areas. . . . As long as there is an interface of products, services, expertise, and technologies between China and the world, this niche will continue to present

and cooperate with each other. A tighter, more dependent relationship continues to develop between the international community and China. Currently, too few parties possess the skills, experience, and knowledge to manage the increasing interests of both sides. A void exists. As long as there is an interface of products, services, expertise, and technologies between China and the world, this niche will continue to present itself and grow.

A unique chance presents itself for Chinese professionals to occupy that middle ground. Bilingual, international-oriented mainlanders should not overlook the chance to participate on an even larger international playing field where they can offer a competitive advantage. The window of opportunity is wide open for those who wish to be facilitators between China and the rest of the world. "Today's generation of mainland professionals could be the critical link to help bring China to the world … or the world to China," proclaims a Chinese entrepreneur stationed in Shanghai. For so many, it is offering an exciting, rewarding, and meaningful place to develop one's career.

图书在版编目(CIP)数据

知己知彼/(美)王承伦著.—北京:中国对外翻译出版公司,2001.6
书名原文:Know The Game, Play The Game
ISBN 7-5001-0886-9

Ⅰ.知… Ⅱ.王… Ⅲ.职业选择-基本知识-英文

Ⅳ.C913.2

中国版本图书馆 CIP 数据核字(2001)第 032311 号

(著作权合同登记:图字 01－2001－1918 号)

出版发行/中国对外翻译出版公司

地　　址/北京市西城区车公庄大街甲 4 号物华大厦六层

电　　话/(010)68002481　68002482

邮　　编/100044

传　　真/(010)68002480

电子邮件/ctpc@public.bta.net.cn

网　　址/www.ctpc.com.cn

规　　格/890×1240　A5

印　　张/7

版　　次/2001 年 8 月第一版

印　　次/2001 年 8 月第一次

印　　数/1－3000

ISBN 7-5001-0886-9/G·248

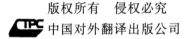